# JOY

## *in*

### *the*

# LORD

Granville M. Williams, S.S.J.E.

PARAMETER PRESS

705 Main Street, Wakefield, Massachusetts 01880, USA

A  ⊣3  ∫  ∞  |  ⇒  ∩  Ω

In the text, hymn numbers refer to
*The Hymnal of the Episcopal Church in the
United States of America, 1940*
published by
The Church Pension Fund, New York.

Library of Congress Catalog Card Number 71-189764
International Standard Book Number 0-88203-001-9

Printed and bound in the United States of America by
The Murray Printing Company
Forge Village, Massachusetts 01828

Composition by
Jane L. Keddy
Wakefield, Massachusetts 01880

# CONTENTS

These retreat addresses
given at various times to the Sisters of
the Society of St. Margaret
are affectionately dedicated to the blessed memory
of
SISTER MARY AGNES, S.S.M.

for many years the wise Superior and the loving Mother of the
American Convent of the Sisterhood.
In response to the hope and desire of Mother Mary Agnes
these addresses are now published
with the prayer that they may prove spiritually helpful
to some who read them.

Chapter 1

## DARKNESS AND LIGHT

*God does not come to us in love because
we are such deserving and nice people, but
because we are sinners.*

### The Darkness of This World

*1 John 5:19   The whole world
lieth in the power of the evil one.*

Yet in many of its aspects this
world in which we live is a place
of beauty and delight.  That is
because the world was created by
God, and the loveliness of its
Maker may still be seen in it.
But in a deeper sense, as St. John
said, "The whole world lieth in
the power of the evil one," in
spiritual darkness.

This darkness is due to the fact
that the world as we know it is a
"fallen" world which has turned
away from its Maker and its God
and has gone its own way in rebellion against the will of God.
It has fallen into sin, into wickedness, into darkness.  Because of
this, a deep sense of tragedy and
sorrow and sadness has entered
into human life.  In spite of all
his efforts to do good and to suc-
ceed, man must face eventually
the certainty of defeat, failure,
incompleteness, darkness, death.

### THE DEVIL'S DIARY

Our daily newspapers plainly
assure us of the reality of this
darkness, that "the whole world
lieth in the power of the evil
one."  The headlines of our
newspapers are, on the whole,
most depressing.  Wars and rumors

1

of wars, crimes, atrocities, corruption, lack of honesty, lack of devotion to truth and right on the part of those chosen to guide and rule the people of the earth—these are largely the subjects of our news. The late Father Huntington of the Order of the Holy Cross used, for this reason, to refer to the newspaper as "the devil's diary," because it is largely the record of the evil which "the prince of this world" has been able to accomplish during the preceding twenty-four hours. Thank God, there are exceptions, of course. Good and noble deeds do sometimes get into the papers, but, on the whole, we must agree that the evil predominates.

THE GOOD AND THE EVIL
IN THE WORLD

As Christians, we cannot hold or believe that the darkness of this world is caused by God. In the account of the creation given in the first chapter of Genesis, the whole point of the narrative is that the Word of God and the Spirit of God bring light out of darkness. "The earth was without form and void; and darkness was upon the face of the deep. . . . And God said, 'Let there be light'; and there was light. And God saw that the light was good" [Genesis 1:2-4].

We notice that at the close of every stage of the creation narrative, "God saw that it was good." Finally we read, "God saw everything that he had made, and behold, it was very good" [Genesis 1:31]. For, as St. John assures us in his first epistle, "God is light, and in him is no darkness at all" [1 John 1:5].

Disobedience to God, the desire on the part of man to have his own way, the desire to grab and to possess at whatever cost, self-will, pride, seeking for selfish pleasures—these are the sources of sin and the causes of the darkness and the wickedness of the world as we know it. These are the things that have plunged the world into darkness and sadness and sorrow. So, when the Savior of the world appeared, when the Son of God was made man, he said, "Lo, I have come to do Thy will, O God" [Hebrews 10:7]. "Not my will, but thine, be done" [Luke 22:42].

When once again God's will is done in this world, then God's light will shine out and overcome the darkness. It is because of the present darkness in the world that St. John writes in his first epistle, "Do not love the world or the things in the world" [1 John 2:15].

The world that we are bidden not to love is the world that has fallen away from God through sin and disobedience, the world that lies in wickedness and darkness, the world under the domination of the evil, "the prince of this world."

The world as created by God, the world which God declared to be very good, the world that is capable of being redeemed and brought back to God—that world is still loved by God and should be loved by us. That is the world of which it is said, "God so loved the world that he gave his only Son, that whoever believes in him should not perish but have eternal life. For God sent the Son into the world, not to condemn the world, but that the world might be saved through him" [John 3:16-17].

Thus the condemnation of the world, that rejection of the world that St. John tells us to make, is a condemnation and rejection of the rebellious world only.

Unfortunately, however, the evil of sin has entered so fully into God's good world that we need to practice great self-restraint, real self-discipline, constant watchfulness in using the things of this fallen world. It becomes necessary in a very real sense for us to learn to die to this world in order to live unto God.

In baptism, St. Paul reminds us, we were baptized into the death of Jesus Christ: "We were buried therefore with him by baptism into death, so that as Christ was raised from the dead by the glory of the Father, we too might walk in newness of life" [Romans 6:4]. And again, "So you also must consider yourselves dead to sin and alive to God in Christ Jesus" [Rom. 6:11]. "Love not the world," in other words, means to die to the fallen world in order that we may be brought into newness of life in God.

In his epistle St. John goes on to tell us that we must overcome "the lust of the flesh and the lust of the eyes and the pride of life" [1 John 2:16]. We must overcome the lust of the flesh, that is to say, the evil desires of self-indulgence arising from our bodily nature that are contrary to the will of God. We must always remember that our bodily nature and our bodily desires are in themselves good and holy and God given. If they are used in accordance with God's will, they are capable of helping us to grow in holiness and in grace.

Then we must renounce the lust of the eyes—the desire of grabbing and getting and using things selfishly with no concern for the rights and happiness of others.

Above all, we must renounce the pride of life—the desire to have our own way, to carry out our own will regardless of the desires or welfare of our neighbors.

CHRISTIAN JOY IN THE WORLD

By renouncing these evil things, we are set free from that wrong love of the world against which St. John warns us. It is thus that, loving God above all things and being conformed to his holy will, we may learn to love the world rightly as God loves it and to use the things of the world safely and, above all, to take our part in helping to bring the world out of darkness by dying to it (yet for it), as Christ himself died to save the world. "Let us then cast off the works of darkness and put on the armor of light" [Romans 13:12].

Finally we remind ourselves that, as St. Paul tells us, we are saved by hope [Romans 8:24]. While it is true that "the whole world lieth in the power of the wicked one," we know also the glorious truth that the light of Christ has shone in the darkness and that Christ, the Light of the world, can save the world and, indeed, has saved the world. Having this hope in Christ and sorrowing for our own sins and failures, we can rise up to walk in the light of Christ and live by the light of Christ in the assurance of salvation through our Lord. "God sent the Son into the world, not to condemn the world, but that the world might be saved through him." If we were "separated from Christ," if we were without God in the world as, alas, so many people are today, then we could have no hope [Ephesians 2:12].

But the Word of God who is the light of the world has been made flesh and has lived our life and has died for us. In Jesus Christ you and I may behold the glory of the only begotten of the father, "full of grace and truth" [John 1:14]. We may indeed behold "the glory of God in the face of Jesus Christ" [2 Corinthians 4:6]. In Jesus Christ, the babe of Bethlehem, in Jesus the man who went about doing good, in the face too of Jesus Christ, dying upon the cross, we behold the glory of God. We behold the redeeming light before which darkness, sin, and death must fade away.

"The world is very evil" [St. Bernard of Cluny, Hymn 595]. But as Christians we cannot be pessimists for we have received the light of Jesus Christ, as old Zechariah prophesied when "filled with the Holy Spirit,"

Through the tender mercy of
  our God
when the day shall dawn upon
  us from on high
to give light to those who sit in
  darkness and in the shadow
  of death,
to guide our feet into the way
  of peace.
  [Luke 1:78-79]

## The Light of the World

*The people who walked in*
*    darkness*
*have seen a great light;*
*those who dwelt in a land of*
*    deep darkness,*
*    on them has light shined.*

             *   *   *

*For to us a child is born,*
*    to us a son is given;*
*and the government will be upon*
*    his shoulder,*
*    and his name will be called*
*"Wonderful Counselor, Mighty*
*    God,*
*    Everlasting Father, Prince of*
*    Peace."         [Isaiah 9:2,6]*

So goes the great messianic prophecy, foretelling the way in
which the Messiah, the Christ,
would come into the world. Into
the darkness of this world there
came the everlasting light when
Jesus was born of Mary at Bethlehem.

St. John tells us that the light
shines in the darkness and that
the darkness has not, for it cannot, overcome it [John 1:5].
Our Lord, having come into the
world, himself speaks to us, "I
am the light of the world; he
that follows me will not walk in
darkness, but will have the light
of life" [John 8:13]. Again, "If
any one walks in the day, he does
not stumble, because he sees the
light of this world" [John 11:9].
This latter saying expresses not
only a truth of nature but also a

supernatural truth. To walk in
the Spirit, we must walk in the
true light of the world: we must
walk in the light of Jesus Christ.
Looking to Jesus, we may walk
securely in the light.

Walking in the light of Christ,
we walk in the spirit of Christ.
Walking in the Spirit, living with
the life of Christ which he imparts to us, we are delivered
from the power of darkness.
Walking in the Spirit, we are able
to live as God would have us live.
"Walk by the Spirit," says St.
Paul, "and do not gratify the desires of the flesh" [Galatians
5:16].

Let us then give thanks to God
for the wonderful deliverance he
has given us in sending to us his
Son, Jesus Christ, the light of the
world, to be our savior. Let us
give "thanks to the Father, who
has qualified us to share in the
inheritance of the saints in light.
He has delivered us from the
dominion of darkness and trans-
ferred us to the kingdom of his
beloved Son" [Colossians
1:12-13].

### LIGHT CAME INTO DARKNESS

With the coming of Christ,
light came into a world of darkness. As Jesus Christ has proclaimed himself to be the light of
the world, so likewise in the Sermon on the Mount he reminds us
that it is our duty also to be the
light of the world [John 8:12;

Matthew 5:14]. Since Christ dwells in our hearts by faith [Ephesians 3:17], that light of the indwelling Christ ought to shine out of our own lives to give light to our fellow men and women. "You are the light of the world. A city set on a hill cannot be hid. Nor do men light a lamp and put it under a bushel, but on a stand, and it gives light to all the house. Let your light so shine before men, that they may see your good works and give glory to your Father who is in heaven" [Matthew 5:14-16].

The proof that we are walking in the light of Christ is that his light shines out from our own lives to bring comfort, help, joy, strength, and gladness to those with whom we come in contact. If we are not bringing anything of the light of Christ to others, then there is something very wrong with our Christian lives.

What Christ calls "our light" is really his light shining in our hearts. It is not really our light at all. So when our light shines before men they are not to glorify us but, rather, our Father in heaven since he is the real source of the light. Let us beware lest in trying to help others we seek to draw them to ourselves and seek their praise of us. Let us rather do all simply in the power of Christ, in the love of God.

The story is told of a missionary meeting in England at which the great Bishop Selwyn of New Zealand shared the platform with a celebrated orator. After the meeting, one who had attended it compared the great orator with the moon, but Bishop Selwyn with the sun. "For," he said, "when the moon shines, we say, 'How beautiful the moon is tonight,' but when the sun shines we thank God for the lovely world in which we live."

Let your light—which is the light of Christ—so shine out into the world of darkness that men may glorify God.

### LIFE CAME INTO DEATH

Then, with the coming of Christ, life came into a world of death. Life, and all the manifestations of life as we know them, are wonderful and beautiful indeed. Yet all life on earth, especially human life as we know it, is imperfect, disappointing, and sad because all must end in incompleteness, frustration, and failure. This is the source of our human tragedy and the subject of much of our greatest literature. All the ephemeral beauty, all the transient loveliness, all the great and noble strivings, must come to an end and pass away, for sin has entered into the world, and "the wages of sin is death. But," as St. Paul immediately goes on to say, "the free gift of God is eternal life [true life, real life, enduring life] in

Christ Jesus our Lord" [Romans 6:23].

"I am the resurrection and the life," said our Lord at the grave of his friend Lazarus. "He who believes in me, though he die, yet shall he live, and whoever lives in me shall never die" [John 11:25-26]. So the coming of Christ into the world has brought the true life, the eternal life into a world of death.

"This is the testimony, that God gave us eternal life, and this life is in his Son. He who has the Son has life; he who has not the Son has not life" [1 John 5:11-12]. Here St. John is not saying that one "who has not the Son of God" does not have any life at all. On the contrary, such a one does have a transient, perishing life. But the enduring, the eternal, life is the gift of the Son of God. Just as we are called upon as Christians to show forth the light of Christ, so too as Christians we are called upon to live in the true, eternal life of Christ, here and now. Even now we are already risen with Christ, and so even now we are to live by and in the true, eternal, heavenly life of Christ.

"If then you have been raised with Christ [since indeed we are even now risen with him, we are to] seek those things that are above, where Christ is, seated at the right hand of God. Set your minds on things that are above, not on things that are on the earth" [Colossians 3:1-2]. So, then, as Christians we must be careful thus to live now in the resurrection life, the eternal life of Christ and of God. So doing, death is vanquished in us. We have passed from death into life. The earthly life will, it is true, come to an end. We shall experience the death of the body. Yet we shall never die, for the eternal life cannot be subject to death.

So we are called upon not only to believe in Christ but to live in Christ. How shall we live this eternal life in Jesus Christ? We shall live in Christ by setting our "minds on things that are above," by practicing the recollection of his presence in our hearts, by striving to do all things in the name, that is, in the power, of the Lord Jesus.

"So you also must consider yourselves dead to sin and alive to God in Christ Jesus" [Romans 6:11].

"It is no longer I who live, but Christ who lives in me" [Galatians 2:20], that is to say, I live in the eternal life, the enduring life, the true life of Jesus Christ.

LOVE CAME INTO HATE

Finally, with the coming of Christ, love came into a world of hate. The world, lying in darkness and separated from God by sin, is a world filled with hatred. That surely requires no argument.

The exaltation of self, the desire to have one's own way regardless of the wishes or happiness of others, envy, jealousy, covetousness—all these lead to those hatreds, cruelties, and injustices which disgrace human life.

God is love. It was God's love for the world which he had made that was the cause of Jesus Christ's coming into the world, in spite of the world's having fallen into sin and darkness. "God so loved the world" that he gave the greatest thing he had. He gave his only begotten Son. He gave himself. God himself came into the world.

God did not wait until the world was worthy of the coming of Christ. God did not wait until the world was worthy of love. If so, Christ could never have come. God sent his Son into a most unworthy and unlovable world. God does not come to us in love (as I fear we sometimes think) because we are such deserving and "nice" people, but because we are sinners. Only his undeserved love can change us into saints. God sent his Son into a most unlovely and unlovable world in order that his own divine and undeserved love might draw some of his children back to the love of the Father.

"In this is love, not that we loved God but that he loved us and sent his Son to be the expiation for our sins. Beloved, if God so loves us, we also ought to love one another [1 John 4:10-11].

Thus it is that Incarnate Love, our Lord Jesus Christ on the eve of his Passion, gives us the new commandment: "A new commandment I give unto you, that you love one another; even as I have loved you, that you also love one another" [John 13:34].

The newness of the commandment does not lie in the demand that we love one another, for we had been told that before. The newness lies in the command to love one another *as he has loved us,* that we love one another in the same way, the same manner, as Jesus Christ has loved us. That, of course, means that we must not wait for people to be attractive or lovable or even deserving of love before our love goes out to them. It means that we must make the effort (sometimes very difficult indeed) to go out to them in patience, in kindness, in gentleness, with constant prayer for them, in the hope that our love may help them to become more lovable. It means that we must be willing also to suffer for them, as Christ suffered for us. It means that we must be willing also to suffer by them, as Christ on the cross loved and

prayed for those who nailed
him there. "Father forgive
them; for they know not what
they do" [Luke 23:34].

This, then, is the great and
new commandment, and this is
the means by which we may pass
from darkness into light.

He who says he is in the light and hates his
brother is in darkness still.        [1 John 2:9]

Beloved, let us love one another; for love is of
God, and he who loves is born of God and
knows God.  He who does not love does not
know God; for God is love.  [1 John 4:7–8]

Chapter 2

*LET NOT YOUR HEARTS*

*BE TROUBLED*

*Few people could look forward with much eagerness
to a life confined to wearing white robes
and golden crowns and to playing upon harps.*

## The Divine Consolation

*John 14:1-3  Let not your
hearts be troubled; believe in
God, believe also in me. In my
Father's house are many rooms;
if it were not so, would I have
told you that I go to prepare a
place for you? And when I go
and prepare a place for you, I
will come again and will take you
to myself, that where I am you
may be also.*

"Let not your hearts be
troubled." At the time that our
Lord spoke these comforting
words to his apostles, there was
certainly a great deal, humanly
speaking, to trouble them. For
Jesus, they had learned, was leaving them. They were facing all
the terrors of an unknown future.
And they would have to face it
alone, without Jesus. How could
this be possible for them without
the help, the consolation, the
strength that they had learned to
find in the presence of Jesus,
their master and their friend?

### THE UNCERTAINTIES OF OUR LIVES

We too have much to trouble
and distress us in the midst of
the uncertainties of the world in
which we have to live. These are

10

times when it seems that most, if not all, of the foundations on which men built their faith and hope in the past seem to be crumbling away. For many, these times seem to be those predicted by our Lord when he spoke of "men fainting with fear and with foreboding of what is coming in the world" [Luke 21:26]. In the midst of these present fears and distresses, our Lord says to us, as he said to the apostles, "Let not your hearts be troubled."

The same consolation which he gave the apostles, he gives to us. "Believe in God, believe also in me." Put your trust in the heavenly Father. Put your trust in me. In effect, our Lord says to them, "You are to believe in me and trust me to the same extent in which you believe and trust in God." He spoke to the apostles as devout Jews who had learned by past experience to trust the God of Israel who had carried them in safety through all the difficulties and tribulations of their past history; who had delivered them from the tyranny of Pharaoh; who had brought them into the Promised Land; and, even after their unfaithfulness and their being led away into captivity in Babylon, had again restored to them their heritage. So the Jews had learned to trust always to God's protective power and God's love, no matter how difficult were the outward circumstances.

This supreme faith and trust is well expressed in the words of Job, "Though he slay me, yet will I trust in him" [Job 13:15, AV]. Even though God seems to be against me, even though he may seem to reject me utterly, my trust in him will not fail. Or, as the Psalmist puts it, "Yea, though I walk through the valley of the shadow of death, I will fear no evil" [Psalm 23:4].

"Just as you believe in the Father, believe also in me." Christ is indeed the strong Son of God. Although we have not seen the Lord with our human eyes as did these apostles, we remember his words to Thomas, "Blessed are those who have not seen and yet believe" [John 20:29]. Our faith in Jesus, if it is true and enduring, can bring to us as great blessings as it did to those who beheld him with their eyes after he had risen. It can, he tells us, bring us even greater blessings.

Strong Son of God, immortal
    Love,
Whom we, that have not seen
    thy face,
By faith, and faith alone,
    embrace,
Believing where we cannot
    prove.
      [Tennyson, Hymn 365]

For "faith is the assurance of things hoped for, the conviction of things not seen" [Hebrews 11:1].

### THE DIFFICULTY OF BELIEVING IN GOD

Yet I wonder sometimes, if our Lord were speaking to us today, might he not reverse the saying and put it in the form, "You believe in me, believe also in God"? Nowadays there are many people who seem to find it difficult, or even impossible, to believe in God. Even Christians, who profess belief in a heavenly Father, often by their thoughts, words, actions seem to indicate that they do not have any *practical* faith in him. Otherwise so much worrying, so much pessimism would surely be impossible for us. We do believe in Jesus and in the love of Jesus and in the goodness of Jesus. But we still find it difficult to believe that God—the supreme reality and power behind the universe—is truly love or that he truly cares for us or watches over us. So Jesus may well be saying to us now, "You believe in me, believe also in God." He reminded Philip, "He who has seen me has seen the Father" [John 14:9]. All that we see in Jesus Christ—his love, his compassion, his goodness—comes from the Father and is in the Father. Because we believe in Jesus, because we believe in God, true and perfect peace will come into our hearts:

Peace, perfect peace, our future all unknown?
Jesus we know, and he is on the throne.
[E. H. Bickersteth, Hymn 436]

### THE RESTING PLACES

Then Jesus goes on to speak of the special place awaiting each one of us in his Father's home. The Authorized Version of the Bible translated the words as "In my Father's house are many mansions," while the Revised Standard Version has "In my Father's house are many rooms." Archbishop Temple, in his *Readings in St. John's Gospel,* has our Lord say, "In my Father's house are many resting-places." The Archbishop comments on this:

> The *resting-places (monai)* are wayside caravanserais— shelters at stops along the road where travellers may rest on their journey. It was the custom in the East . . . for travellers to send a dragoman forward to make preparation in the next of those resting-places along the road, so that when they came they might find in it comfort as well as shelter. Here the Lord presents himself as our spiritual dragoman, who treads the way of faith before us . . . and makes ready to welcome us [p. 226].

Our Lord has gone ahead and prepared everything for us on

the way. Our future is quite secure. Even here on earth, he has prepared the days that lie ahead of us, and he has prepared for us all things in the life of the world to come. We must never forget that the life of the world to come is real life. So much of the world's sorrow arises from the belief that our life is limited to life in this world. The cynical conclusion follows, as St. Paul points out, "Let us eat and drink, for tomorrow we die" [1 Corinthians 15:32]. But our Lord has assured us, "Whoever lives and believes in me shall never die" [John 11:26].

Also St. Paul tells us that the better life is that of the world to come. "For me to live [i. e., 'in the flesh'] is Christ, and to die is gain. . . . My desire is to depart and be with Christ, for that is far better" [Philippians 1:21, 23].

"In my Father's house are many resting-places." These words lead us to consider the possibility of progress still to be made in the world to come. Furthermore, here in this world as pilgrims we must be making progress. Our spiritual life, our life in Christ, can never stand still. Every day Christ prepares a new resting-place for us. Let us rejoice in it, not mourning for the old resting-place, but accepting the new one that our Lord this day has prepared for us.

## REALITY VS. SYMBOLS

Then too, the many mansions or resting-places may speak to us of the infinite opportunities, infinite adaptabilities, infinite joys of that glorious heavenly life. The glory of heaven is one—the glory which comes from God and from the Lamb of God, our Lord Jesus Christ. Yet that one glory, streaming from God and from the Lamb, comes with infinite possibilities of adaptation to each, so that each will find a peculiar and individual joy in the glory that is common to all. No matter what our individual tastes and backgrounds may be here, there each one will find joy and satisfaction and happiness. We must not mistake for realities the images and symbols, even Biblical ones, that are used to describe the life of heaven. Few people nowadays—perhaps few in any age—could look forward with much eagerness to a life confined to wearing white robes and golden crowns and to playing upon harps. The true joy of heaven is to be found in the presence of God and the experience of the glory of God, "I saw no temple in the city, for its temple is the Lord God the Almighty and the Lamb. And the city has no need of sun or moon to shine upon it, for the glory of God is its light, and its lamp is the Lamb" [Revelation 21:22, 23].

In the vision of God's glory we shall find all that is beautiful, all that is good, all that is truly desirable. "Every good endowment and every perfect gift" which we may encounter during our earthly pilgrimage "is from above, coming down from the Father of lights" [James 1:17]. Every true joy, every lovely thing exists in him, and is to be found in him. "Late have I loved thee, O beauty so ancient and so new, late have I loved thee!" wrote St. Augustine in his *Confessions* [bk. 10, chap. 27]. He thus expressed his regret in having sought during his early years the truly beautiful and desirable in creatures, rather than in God himself.

Our Lord himself, then, prepares for us our daily resting-places here on earth, as well as our eternal home in heaven. Although this is so, let us not forget that we too have our part to play in the preparation. "We are fellow workmen for God" [1 Corinthians 3:9]. Let us ask the Holy Spirit in the days that lie ahead to help us to build up those precious things which will endure eternally in heaven.

When all is ready, our Savior tells us, "I will come again and take you to myself" [John 14:3]. "I will come again." We must never lose sight of the truth that our Savior will come again to us. Indeed he comes again to us repeatedly because of his love for us. He came to Bethlehem as a little child; he came to Jerusalem on Palm Sunday to manifest himself as the promised Messiah; we look for his final coming in glory, at the consummation of the age, to be our judge.

### CHRIST AND THE EVENTS OF HISTORY

These are not the only comings of Jesus Christ, however. He truly comes again in all the events of our troubled world, in every crisis of history. Indeed, the word *crisis* literally means *judgment*. Christ as judge comes continually in the events of history. He comes in judgment and also in blessing in the varied events of our personal lives. He will come again at the end of our earthly life, to take us to himself. When he then comes, shall I be ready? Do I pray day by day, "Come, Lord Jesus"?

"I will come again and will take you to myself, that where I am you may be also." That is the promise, that is the hope—the promise and hope of joy and glory. "That where I am you may be also." And where is our Lord Jesus? "He is in heaven." Yes, he is in heaven. And where is heaven; Heaven is wherever the Lord Jesus is. So, as the poet says, "Where he is in the heart, city of God, thou art" [F. T. Palgrave, Hymn 491]. Heaven can be in our hearts if Jesus is in our hearts.

Even here on earth, our citizenship is in heaven [Philippians 3:20]. "If then you have been raised with Christ, seek the things that are above. . . . Set your minds on things that are above, not on things that are on the earth" [Colossians 3:1, 2]. "Let not your hearts be troubled" [John 14:1]. "Look up and raise your heads, because your redemption is drawing near" [Luke 21:28]. "'Surely I am coming soon.' Amen. Come, Lord Jesus!" [Revelation 22:20].

## The Divine Promises

*John 14:4, 9, 12 "You know the way where I am going. . . . He who has seen me has seen the Father. . . . He who believes in me will also do the works that I do; and greater works than these will he do, because I go to the Father."*

### HOW CAN WE KNOW THE WAY?

Yes, we do know the way, although perhaps we may feel tempted to say with Thomas, "Lord, we do not know where you are going; how can we know the way?" [John 14:5]. Since our final heavenly destination is still unknown to us and the

vision of God has not yet dawned upon us, how can we know the way to an unknown place? The answer given by our Lord is that we do not need to know the *place;* it is enough to know the *way.* If we follow the way, we shall reach our destination. "This is the way, walk in it" [Isaiah 30:21]. This is the way to heaven. The way of life to which we have been called by God, our particular calling or vocation (if we have sought God's will for us), that is our road to heaven. By walking in the way, we walk with Jesus and in Jesus. He goes on to assure us of this, "I am the way, the truth, and the life" [John 14:6].

The Christian life is often referred to as the Imitation of Christ. In fact, the great devotional classic by à Kempis is usually given that title. But the purpose of our lives as Christians is not to try to reproduce in our lives the same conditions and actions as those that marked the life of Jesus. To walk in the way of Christ is not even to follow after him, although in a sense that forms part of it. To walk in the way of Christ rather means to walk *in him,* in the power of his Spirit, letting his Spirit work in us and through us, directing and controlling our lives. The actual conditions of our life will almost certainly be entirely

different from those of our
Lord's earthly life. If we walk
in him, though, we shall ourselves
be living the Christ life—here and
now. "I am the true and living
way."

He will not ask us to go
through any greater difficulties
or dangers or temptations than
he himself has experienced and
conquered. There is no part of
the way which is so dark and
fearful but that you may pass
through it safely if only you
put your hand into the hand of
Jesus Christ.

To walk in the way—to walk in
Christ—is not to walk in a path
always abounding in pleasures.
We shall, of course, experience
many outward joys as well as
inward consolations as we go on
in this true and living way. We
must not forget, however, that
the way followed by our Lord led
up to Calvary. "Far be it from
me to glory," says St. Paul, "except in the cross of our Lord
Jesus Christ, by which the world
has been crucified to me, and I
to the world" [Galatians 6:14].
To glory in the cross is to rejoice
when the cross enters into our
lives. The way of the cross is, at
the same time, the way of life,
the way to the Father, the way
to heaven. "No one comes to
the Father, but by me" [John
14:6], that is, by walking in me,
"the way, and the truth, and the
life."

Let us then rejoice that our
feet have been set in this, the
true and right way. Of Jesus it is
written, "for the joy that was set
before him [he] endured the
cross, despising the shame"
[Hebrews 12:2]. Pray that our
Lord may reveal to us also the
mysterious joys of the way of
the holy cross, our one sure way
to God.

WHAT IS GOD LIKE?

In the second of these divine
promises, Christ assures us, "He
who has seen me has seen the
Father" [John 14:9]. "Blessed
are the pure in heart, for they
shall see God" [Matthew 5:8].
To see God is the ultimate goal
of human life—the very purpose
for which we have been created.
If we are able to see God, we
shall experience the divine comfort, we shall know that all is
well. To see God is to enable
ourselves to see as God sees. In
spite of sins, of difficulties, of all
the troubles that are now in the
world, God, who sees the whole,
nevertheless knows even now
that all is well. While he beholds
all the sorrows, still he knows the
perfect joy. Beyond the cross,
our Lord beheld "the joy that
was set before him." The ultimate attainment is the joy. The
ultimate reality is triumph—
victory.

In Genesis we read, "God saw
everything that he had made, and

behold it was very good" [Genesis 1:31]. God still sees all that he has made, and, in a mystery, behold, it is still very good. For the power of God can bring good out of evil. So the day that our Lord died upon the Cross, the day that marks the culmination of man's sin, is rightly called Good Friday by the Church. In God's presence, "there is fulness of joy" [Psalm 16:11].

In a very real sense, we have already seen the Father: "No one has ever seen God; the only Son, who is in the bosom of the Father, he has made him known" [John 1:18]. While no man has seen, or can see, God in his inmost essence, we have seen Jesus with the eyes of faith. In thus seeing Jesus, we have truly seen the Father. God, as he can be known by us, cannot be different from Jesus Christ. Jesus is full of tender love and sympathy, deep understanding, readiness to forgive. God is like that. Jesus has a stern side too. He has no patience with selfishness, with self-centeredness, with lack of the spirit of forgiveness. God too is like that. "If you forgive men their trespasses, your heavenly Father also will forgive you; but if you do not forgive men their trespasses, neither will your Father forgive your trespasses" [Matthew 6:14, 15].

So, if we would know the love of Jesus, we must ask our Lord to give us his forgiving Spirit. We must try to understand and overlook the faults of others and take them into our hearts, even as the sacred compassionate heart of Jesus embraces all mankind. "Be merciful," for the merciful servant alone obtained mercy. "Judge not," if you would escape the judgment of God. "Condemn not, and you will not be condemned; forgive and you will be forgiven" [Luke 6:36, 37]. While all the wonder of God's love is seen in Jesus, the need for a merciful, forgiving spirit is also seen in him.

We who have seen Jesus have seen the Father in him. "We have beheld his glory, glory as of the only Son from the Father" [John 1:14]. So we pray to him: O gracious Lord Jesus, show us the Father, show us thyself. Reveal thyself to us more and more. Teach us to behold the glory of God in thine own adorable face, so that all faithless fears, dread forebodings, and baseless sorrows may vanish away. Show us the Father, and we shall be satisfied. Show us the Father, for that is all we need. In that vision, we shall find rest, peace, and joy.

### HOW CAN WE DO GREAT WORKS?

The third of the divine promises of Christ is, "He who believes in me will also do the works that I do" [John 14:12]. Not only does he promise that we shall do his works. He goes on to declare that we shall be enabled to do "greater works than these," because he has gone to the Father and from thence pours out on us in abundance his Holy Spirit. As he told his disciples after his resurrection, "All authority in heaven and on earth has been given to me, Go ye therefore," endued with this same supreme authority [Matthew 28:18, 19]. In his supreme power and by his supreme authority, we shall do his works.

Very likely his works that are to be accomplished by us will not be as outwardly spectacular as some of the works he did during his life on earth. Nevertheless he declared that they would be "greater works." We shall not heal lepers by a touch or by a word, we shall not turn water into wine, but we remember that in the Fourth Gospel, the mighty works of Christ are always called "signs." The outward miracles are but signs of the more wonderful divine love operating in and through them. Every operation of the Holy Spirit, every showing forth of divine love, is a true miracle. These are the wonderful works of Christ that you and I are called upon to do.

The Christian disciple who lives and walks in the spirit of love, who truly loves his neighbor, who is patient, tolerant, gentle, and kind, is truly performing the works of Christ. He or she will not secure great publicity because of this. But these disciples are truly beloved of Christ. "He who believes in me will also do the works that I do." Such disciples will show forth the miracle of a Christlike life of love.

Moreover, we shall find that our prayers are answered. "Whatever you ask in my name, I will do it" [John 14:13]. We must be careful to ask *in his name,* according to his will of holy love. Alas! That we should ever allow ourselves to ask anything contrary to his name, contrary to his holy loving will. But if we ask for anything in his name, he will do it, and, as we ask, our wills are brought into harmony with his divine will. As we ask in his name, we shall experience the blessings and wonders of the saintly life. The miracles of the saints may be ours now if our hearts, like theirs, are truly surrendered in trustful love to Jesus Christ, our Lord.

### THE CHRISTIAN'S WORK

What we are called upon to do as Christians is, above all, to demonstrate Christ's power of love in the midst of a world of

hate.  In the midst of an
unbelieving world, we are to
demonstrate the power of faith
through prayer.  In the midst of
a world which more and more
seems to rely on the power of
brute force, Christians are to arm
themselves with "the sword of
the Spirit, which is the word of
God," praying "at all times in
the Spirit" [Ephesians 6:17, 18].

If you ask anything in my name, I will do it.
[John 14:13]

If God is for us, who is against us?
[Romans 8:31]

All things are yours . . . whether . . . the world
or life or death or the present or the future, all
are yours; and you are Christ's; and Christ is
God's.          [1 Corinthians 3:21, 22]

Chapter 3

## JOY IN THE LORD

*What we call love is often only the attempt to
grab and possess something that gives us
pleasure, to be kept and used as long as it
satisfies and then to be cast away as useless.*

### Christian Joy

*Philippians 4:4-5   Rejoice in the
Lord always; again I will say,
Rejoice. Let all men know
your forbearance. The Lord is
at hand.*

A characteristic of the
Christian religion is its joyous-
ness. Gloom and depression and
pessimism are as much opposed
to our holy religion as darkness
is to light. Not, of course, that
we as Christians are called upon
to shut our eyes to the sin and
evil and troubles of the world
about us. Rather, beholding and
acknowledging the presence of
all these evil things, we still hold
fast in faith to the truth that

20

Christ has won the victory and that, in the end, these things will be overcome.

THE SOURCE OF
OUR JOY

Beyond this, the Christian looks to the presence of Jesus Christ in his heart and in his life as the source of an enduring and abiding joy. Christ born once in human form on the first Christmas day, is mystically reborn in the heart of the believer through the sacrament of Holy Baptism; and Christ in the heart is nourished and grows daily in each of us through prayer and through Holy Communion. This knowledge that God is truly with us should lead us on to inward and constant rejoicing. As the Apostle puts it in those striking words in Ephesians, "Do not get drunk with wine, for that is debauchery; but be filled with the Spirit, addressing one another in psalms and hymns and spiritual songs, singing and making melody to the Lord with all your heart, always and for everything giving thanks in the name of our Lord Jesus Christ to God the Father" [Ephesians 5:18-20].

"Rejoice in the Lord, and again I say, Rejoice." Jesus Christ the Lord is the source of our joy. Alas, that so many of our fellow men and women should be led by the spiritual enemy of the human race to try to find true joy and happiness in anything outside of Jesus the Lord, for this is a vain attempt. The frantic search for happiness in passing worldly joys, in material good, in sensual indulgence, in restless distractions, or even, on a higher plane, in intellectual pursuits or in human friendships and human love—all this is a disheartening symptom of the hopelessness of an age which has forgotten Christ and is lost in a meaningless universe.

So St. Paul, writing to Christian converts, reminds them of their sad and joyless state before the mercy of God brought them to Christ the Savior. "Remember that you were at that time separated from Christ, . . . and strangers to the covenants of promise, having no hope and without God in the world" [Ephesians 2:12]. That is the condition of many of our fellow men today. They deserve far more our compassion and our prayers than our scorn and contempt.

How greatly, then, should we rejoice in the Lord—in Jesus Christ. How thankful we ought to be that "in the fulness of time" God in his great love sent his Son into the world, to take away the burden of our sins, to take away our sorrow and sadness, and to make it possible for us in every circumstance of life, no matter how dark and difficult things may look, to rejoice because, on that first Christmas day, Jesus Christ came into the world. "To us a child is born, to us a son is given; . . . and his name shall be called Wonderful Counselor, Mighty God, Everlasting Father, Prince of Peace" [Isaiah 9:6].

### THE REALITY OF OUR RELIGION

Then, as we rejoice in Jesus, we must strive to become like Jesus. "Let your forbearance, your kindness, your patience, be known unto all men." Not to just a few men, whom we happen to like, but to all men. We must go out in patience and kindness to all with whom we come in contact, not merely to those whom we happen to like or admire. Christ dwelling in our hearts by faith must be allowed to manifest that inward presence in our outward lives, by our words, by our actions. Yes, even by our thoughts! If we are not thus manifesting him—in our lives, in our thoughts, words, and actions—we are only deceiving ourselves about the reality of our religion. As Christians, we must take great care never to be domineering, contentious, quarrelsome, or selfish; but always we must be going out to others in love and sympathy; always we must be considerate of others, of their feelings, and of their points of view.

In the Epistle to the Galatians, St. Paul enumerates for us the ninefold fruit of the Holy Spirit who brings forth in our lives "love, joy, peace, patience, kindness, goodness, faithfulness, gentleness, self-control" [Galatians 5:22]. It is this fruit of the Spirit, he is telling us here, that should be made evident to all those with whom we come in contact.

### TO UNDERSTAND WHAT LOVE REALLY IS

"Have this mind among yourselves, which you have in Christ Jesus, who, though he was in the form of God, did not count equality with God a thing to be grasped, but emptied himself, taking the form of a servant, being born in the likeness of men" [Philippians 2:5-7]. "For us men and for our salvation he came down from heaven." That, of course, does not mean that he traveled from one *place* to another *place*. "He came down from heaven," means rather, as St. Paul puts it, "he emptied himself."

He exchanged his state of glory for a state of humiliation. For the love of us, he let the glory go. "He came down," he humbled himself and became man, like one of us, one with us. Love and love alone "brought him down from heaven to be born as a little child in Bethlehem. If we would enter truly into the mystery of Christmas, we must try to understand what love really is.

With us, what we call 'love' is very often only a word designating the attempt to grab and possess something that gives us pleasure, to be kept and used as long as it satisfies our own selfish desire and then to be cast away as useless. That is not real love. That is not Christian love. That is not the way that God showed his love to us in Christ. Our Lord came down from heaven not because we were good or beautiful or desirable or in any way worthy of his love. He came when we had spurned and rejected the love of God. He came to us as sinners. He did not come to us because, as we are often tempted to think, we are "such nice people." Christ came because we had rejected God, because we had lost God. He came so that, by showing God's mercy and pity and loving kindness, he might draw us back again into this boundless love which is God.

Through the beauty that we glimpse in Jesus as he grew up on earth, through his own forbearance, his kindness, his pity, his sweet reasonableness, we are drawn more and more to him, and so to the love of God. We must then try to express in our own lives the things that are so beautiful in our Lord's character. We must learn not to be too insistent on our own rights or too demanding on others or what we think is justly due to us. Let these things go! They are truly of no real importance. But cling fast to the love of God.

### A MONUMENT TO IMPERFECT FAITH

"The Lord is at hand." As our Lord came to this earth once at the first Christmas, so our Christian faith tells us that "he shall come again, with glory." For the believer, this second coming of Christ in glory cannot be a source of dread. Rather, as is made plain here, its expectation is a source of joy. "Rejoice in the Lord, *because* the Lord is at hand." That longing for his coming is made very plain, in almost the final words of our Bible, "He who testifies to these things says, 'Surely I am coming soon.' Amen. Come, Lord Jesus!" [Revelation 22:20].

It is only those who do not wish to know or love or serve the Lord Jesus who can ever regard the coming of Christ with terror or fear. The medieval hymn *Dies Irae,* in spite of its wonderful poetic imagery, is a monument to imperfect faith and a misunderstanding of the second coming of our Lord. That other medieval hymn of Bernard of Cluny, *Hora Novissima,* is far more truly Christian. It begins, as you know, in the translation made by John Mason Neale [Hymn 595] :

> The world is very evil;
>   The times are waxing late;
> Be sober and keep vigil;
>   The Judge is at the gate:
> The Judge that comes in mercy,
>   The Judge that comes with
>     might,
> To terminate the evil,
>   To diadem the right.

The Judge who comes is one with the Babe of Bethlehem, the merciful Savior who gave himself for us on the cross. He comes in mercy to take away all the evil, sin, and wickedness of the world and to diadem the right, to crown all those who have desired to love and follow him and to receive them into his heavenly kingdom. When and exactly how this final coming of Christ in glory will take place, no one knows. He himself has told us, "But of that day or that hour no one knows, not even the angels in heaven, nor the Son, but only the Father" [Mark 13:32]. Nevertheless, it is true always that "The Lord is at hand" to redeem and save and help us. "Look up and raise your heads, because your redemption is drawing near" [Luke 21:28].

So he will be with us in the days that lie ahead, upholding us in every hour of trial or need according to his promise, "Lo, I am with you always, to the close of the age" [Matthew 28:20]. We may be quite sure that he will not leave us even in the hour of death, for "The Lord is my shepherd, I shall not want; . . . though I walk through the valley of the shadow of death, I will fear no evil: for thou art with me" [Psalm 23:1, 4].

Finally, the time will come when we shall say, "The Kingdom of the world has become the kingdom of our Lord and of his Christ, and he shall reign for ever and ever" [Revelation 11:15].

## Christian Peace

*Philippians 4:6– 7   Have no anxiety about anything, but in everything by prayer and supplication with thanksgiving let your requests be made known to God. And the peace of God, which passes all understanding, will keep your hearts and your minds in Christ Jesus.*

"Have no anxiety about anything." That, of course, is exactly what our Lord taught us in the Sermon on the Mount. "Do not be anxious about tomorrow. . . . Do not be anxious, saying, 'What shall we eat?' or 'What shall we drink?' or 'What shall

we wear?' " [Matthew 6:34, 31].
Jesus mentions the very necessi-
ties of life—food, drink, and
clothing—without which we cannot live. He tells us that we are
not to be anxious, we are not to
worry even, about these things.

### THE ESCAPE FROM ANXIETY

Then he goes on to tell us how
we are to escape from being
anxious. "Seek first his [your
heavenly Father's] kingdom and
his righteousness, and all these
things shall be yours as well"
[Matthew 6:33]. Seek first of
all God's kingdom. Make sure
that your aims are right. Get
your values straightened out.
Make your religion real.

Our Lord does not counsel us
to give most of our energies and
thought to seeking material
things, even necessary material
things. Our Lord does not advise
us to devote most of our efforts
and attention to amassing money
and seeking material security and
pursuing pleasure. Then, when
all these aims have been accomplished, if we still have left over
a little energy and a little time
that we can devote to God and
his kingdom, that will be all
right. He tells us nothing of the
kind. He says instead to seek
first of all the kingdom of God
and his righteousness, or justice.

The saints of all ages have
taken Christ at his word, have
put the kingdom of God first.
They have found that their needs
are indeed supplied and that God
brings into their lives real joy,
real happiness, and real serenity.

"Have no anxiety about anything." We read in the gospels
of the time when the apostles
were fearfully tossed about in a
little boat by wind and storm as
they were crossing the Lake of
Galilee. In terror they went to
Jesus, asleep in the stern of the
boat, and awoke him. They even
reproached him as if he did not
care about them. "Teacher, do
you not care if we perish?"
(Sometimes, I am afraid, we
behave in the same way to
Jesus.) After he had calmed the
tempest by a word, he said to
the disciples, "Why are you
afraid? Have you no faith?"
[Mark 4:36–40].

"Cast all your anxieties on
him," says St. Peter, "for he
cares about you" [1 Peter 5:7].
All fears, all anxieties, all worries
would be done away if we could
realize and truly believe the great
truth that God has loved us and
does love us with an everlasting,
an eternal, love.

The first article of our Christian creed is, "I believe in God
the Father Almighty." That is
to say, "I believe that he whom
we call God is an Almighty
Father; I believe that the great
directing power behind the uni-

verse, the great and ultimate reality in and behind the universe, is not a blind, impersonal, meaningless force; but one who can be described in personal terms as a Father, an Almighty Father, an all-powerful Father."

Because of this belief, St. Paul can say, "We know that in everything God works for good with those who love him" [Romans 8:28]. Our love for God rises out of the prior love of God for us. "In this the love of God was made manifest among us, that God sent his only Son into the world, so that we might live through him. In this is love, not that we loved God but that he loved us and sent his Son to be the expiation for our sins" [1 John 4:9–10].

IF GOD KNOWS OUR NEEDS, WHY PRAY?

With this confidence in God's love and help and care for us, we turn to him, praying in trust for all our needs. "In everything by prayer and supplication with thanksgiving let your requests be made known to God" [Philippians 4:6].

If we would have God's help, we must ask for it. It is true, of course, as our Lord reminds us, that "Your father knows what you need before you ask him" [Matthew 6:8]. Nevertheless, we are still to ask. To pray, to ask God to give us what we need,

this is a law of the spiritual life. We must turn to our heavenly Father and make our requests known to him with the trustful confidence of a little child. "Ask, and it will be given to you; seek, and you will find; knock, and it will be opened to you. For every one who asks receives, and he who seeks finds, and to him who knocks it will be opened" [Matthew 7:7–8].

This relationship that we take toward God, as trustful children of a loving Father is what we mean by the life of prayer. It is absolutely essential if we would know the joy of the Lord and if we would have that sure faith in his love to us which banishes all care and anxiety.

We could not expect to maintain our bodily health and strength without regular times for food and rest. We could not live at all if we stopped breathing. Prayer is truly the breathing of the soul, and without prayer our spiritual life will perish. In all details of our life, in all our joys and in all our trials, we need to turn to God in prayer. Sometimes indeed we turn to him in wordless prayer, the simple "looking unto Jesus" which will bring us new courage, new hope, new strength. St. Paul expresses the same thoughts when he writes in the first epistle to the Thessalonians, "Rejoice always, pray constantly, give thanks in all circumstances; for this is the will of God in Christ Jesus for you" [1 Thessalonians 5:16-18].

Our life of prayer then, if it is to be really Christian, must rest upon the foundation of constant praise and thanksgiving to God for all his love, all his mercies, all his beauty. As we approach him in loving faith to ask him to supply our present needs, we must come with grateful hearts for all the mercies and blessings that he has given us in the past. It is easy to get into the habit of dwelling exclusively on the difficulties and pains and troubles of life. The result is that we come to overlook almost completely the joys and blessings which are always there too and which have been bestowed so abundantly on us in the past.

A CHRISTIAN DANGER SIGNAL

It is always a bad sign, spiritually speaking, when we begin to allow ourselves to feel sorry for ourselves, whatever the cause. That is a real danger signal to the Christian life.

Why should we feel sorry for ourselves ever? In the midst of a world where so many people know nothing of our Lord, nothing of God, we have been brought into the Church, we have received and continue to receive the sacraments, we have the assurance that Jesus himself dwells in our hearts and lives

through the power of the Holy Spirit. How wonderful this all is!

Surely these joys alone should fill us with thanksgiving, not to mention all the other natural joys—lovely things in the world around us, treasures of art, and science, our homes, our friends, our families, all the precious and beautiful things that we have known and experienced during our earthly lives. All of these, let us not forget, come from God. "Every good endowment and every perfect gift is from above, coming down from the Father of lights" [James 1:17]. Take the trouble to draw up a Catalog of Lovely Things, a list— it can be only partial and imperfect—of all the many things you have, or have had, for which you should give thanks to God. When you are tempted to feel depressed, to give way to self-pity, take a look at this Catalog of Lovely Things. Try to make every day a Thanksgiving Day.

PEACE? IN THESE TIMES!

Finally, in response to our life of joy in the Lord and to our turning to God in trustful prayer, the peace of God will surely come to us to calm all the inward tumults of our souls.

"Love, joy, peace." These are bracketed together by St. Paul as the first three characteristics of the fruit of the Holy Spirit. Our joy in the Lord and our love for God exhibited by our trust in his care and goodness, these bring into our lives that peace of God which passes all understanding [Philippians 4:7].

Peace is one of the blessings that our world is eagerly seeking and desiring. The world, alas, seems unlikely to find peace because it does not understand the nature of true peace. The world looks for peace in the wrong places and seeks to bring it about by the wrong means. The history of the world follows a sad pattern of "times of war" and "times of peace" endlessly repeated. But the so-called times of peace are not really times of peace at all. They are only interludes or breathing spaces to enable the rival powers to catch their breath and prepare themselves for the next show of force in war. The world itself seems finally to have realized that this is the truth, so that wars are no longer followed by peace, but rather "hot" wars are followed by "cold" wars. Wars, therefore, really never stop. Peace never really comes.

The peace of God "which passes all understanding" is not a cold war but a real peace, a condition in which all the seemingly opposed and conflicting interests of human life are caught up and harmonized and unified in and by the great overruling love of Christ Jesus our King. To allow Christ to rule our lives, really to

rule them, is to know the joy of an enduring peace in the heart and soul and mind. Only as the nations of this world come likewise to accept, at least in some measure, the rule of Christ the King, can they, in turn, find true peace.

The peace of God will truly come to us always if we can surrender ourselves in trustful love to the rule of Christ the King. We then shall be at peace, even though the world is not at peace. We shall be free from inward conflicts, distresses, fears. If we are truly men and women of good will, if we are truly seeking to put away hatred, suspicion, envy, and jealousy, then there will be fulfilled in us the promise given in the angelic message on the first Christmas day, "Glory to God in the highest, and on earth peace among men with whom he is pleased!" [Luke 2:14].

Since it proceeds from the love of Christ himself, this peace of God guards and protects our hearts and minds in Christ Jesus [Philippians 4:7]. Our whole inner being, our whole life, our emotions, our affections, our wills, and our thoughts are the objects of God's constant care and protection. As St. Paul says, "If God is for us who is against us?" [Romans 8:31]. If God is on our side, what matter who is on the other?

But we need to cooperate with God. We need to be watchful. "Blessed," said Jesus in the sixth of those Beatitudes that open the Sermon on the Mount, "Blessed are the pure in heart, for they shall see God" [Matthew 5:8]. Not only must goodness, love, and purity mark our outward life, but we need to be watchful to keep our thoughts worthy of the Lord who, by faith, dwells in our hearts. Indeed the disciplining of our thoughts will determine inevitably the content of our words and the nature of our actions. We cannot, of course, by ourselves keep our hearts and minds focused on the knowledge and love of God and of his Son, Jesus Christ our Lord. But the peace of God as it comes to us, and as we realize that it has come and thank God for it, will bring about this result.

Joy in the Lord; forbearance and love towards our neighbor; watchfulness and eager waiting for Christ's coming; putting away every anxious care; turning to God in loving trust; keeping ourselves in a state of thankfulness for God's many blessings— these will surely bring into our lives the peace of God, which passes understanding and will keep our hearts and minds grounded and rooted in the love of Christ Jesus.

Finally, brethren, whatever is true, whatever is honorable, whatever is just, whatever is pure, whatever is lovely, whatever is gracious, if there is any excellence, if there is anything worthy of praise, think about these things. What you have learned and received and heard and seen in me, do; and the God of peace will be with you.

[Philippians 4:8-9]

Chapter 4

## THE CROSS AND THE CROWN

*The attempt to avoid pain*
*at any cost and in every possible way*
*has led to frightful evils in the world.*

### The Cross

*Hebrews 12:11  For the moment all discipline seems painful rather than pleasant; later it yields the peaceful fruit of righteousness to those who have been trained by it.*

The purpose of difficulties, of trouble, of discipline in our lives is to teach us to "sit lightly" to outward things, to learn detachment from the world and the things of this world, and so to prepare us for the joys of the heavenly life. Besides acts of voluntary self-discipline (fasting, etc.) which we may be called upon to practice in our lives as Christians, there are the many involuntary difficulties, disappointments, or sufferings —great or small—which all of us have to encounter day by day.

These circumstances of life, circumstances which lie beyond our control, are sometimes referred to by theologians as "the will of God's good pleasure," referring to St. Paul's words in Philippians, "God is at work in you, both to will and work for his good pleasure" [Philippians 2:13]. "We know that in everything God works for good with those who love him" [Romans 8:28], which means that these difficult and painful things that

30

come to us in life are intended by our heavenly Father for our ultimate good, as well as are the pleasant and agreeable things. Let us ask our Lord, then, to help us to accept, not merely with resignation but even with the thankfulness which comes from our trusting faith, all the difficulties, the sorrows, the troubles, the weaknesses and the sufferings which may come to us in our lives here on earth.

HOW CAN A
GOOD GOD ALLOW SUFFERING?

We cannot, of course, help wishing that these troubles might leave us because we know that absence of pain and difficulty does bring a certain natural happiness and joy into life; but very often God draws souls close to himself by suffering. One way to be near Jesus is to be near the cross and share the pain of Jesus. Indeed suffering and trouble may be very helpful in keeping us close to God. The Psalmist says, "Before I was afflicted I went astray: but now I keep thy word." Without difficulties or sufferings, I missed the path, but now I know that these very difficulties are means that God is using to help me keep his word.

Let us pray that we may learn, then, to be "patient in tribulation" [Romans 12:12]. Indeed, even beyond this patience, St.

Paul tells us, "We rejoice in our sufferings, knowing that suffering produces endurance, and endurance produces character, and character produces hope, and hope does not disappoint us, because God's love has been poured into our hearts through the Holy Spirit which has been given to us" [Romans 5:3-5]. "Christ also suffered for you, leaving you an example, that you should follow in his steps" [1 Peter 2:21].

As Christians we are called upon to follow in the steps of Christ, to take up our cross daily and follow him [Matthew 16:24]. This is the universal Christian vocation: as Christians we must expect and accept hardships, difficulties, sufferings. Great saints have had to endure terrible persecutions, even martyrdom. When we think of what they suffered for Christ, most of our sufferings must seem very small.

Ananias was sent by the Lord to the newly converted Saul, with the message, "I will show him how much he must suffer for the sake of my name" [Acts 9:16]. A partial catalog of those sufferings has been given to us by St. Paul himself in the eleventh chapter of Second Corinthians verses 23 to 29. Included among them, along with shipwreck and beatings, is the sorrow of being betrayed by false friends and the overburdening anxiety that came to him with "the care of all the churches."

Our Lord tells us, "A disciple is not above his teacher, nor the servant above his master: it is enough for the disciple to be like his teacher, and the servant like his master" [Matthew 10:24-25]. We then must be like Jesus Christ and like St. Paul and the other saints. It is a necessary part of our vocation.

### NOT THAT KIND OF CROSS!

Since it is necessary if we would follow Jesus to take up our cross, we must not be surprised and complaining when the cross comes. The trouble is that, while we expect a cross, we have figured out just what sort of cross it is going to be. The cross that comes to us, however, is of quite a different kind. We must try to greet it when it comes, no matter how strange its shape. According to tradition, St. Andrew, like our Lord, was crucified. But the shape of St. Andrew's cross was different from that of our Lord's. It was an X cross, not a T cross. But St. Andrew did not reject it because of its unexpected shape. We are told that he greeted it, instead, with the words, "O welcome cross! Receive the disciple of him who hung on thee, my master, Christ. A cross made holy by his body, and blessed by its burden!"

There is a miracle of divine love by which sorrow is turned into joy [John 16:20]. Some of the great saints, as we know, have not only welcomed the sufferings which came to them day by day but have even sought them out in order to be closer to Jesus by sharing his cross. In this they were not looking for those perverse physical joys in suffering against which modern psychologists warn us. The saints found no joy in the cross in that sense. Neither did Christ. On the contrary, we know that his human nature shrank from the cross and all the suffering surrounding it, even with the utmost terror, which is the meaning of the agony in the garden. "My Father, if it be possible, let this cup pass from me; nevertheless, not as I will, but as thou wilt" [Matthew 26:39]. He did not find in the garden, nor on Calvary, any pleasure of the senses, but he did experience that deep, miraculous joy of mind and spirit in knowing that he was submitting to the will of the Father—the will which is always holy, loving, and good.

So in the discourse of the Last Supper, Jesus says to the disciples, "Truly, Truly, I say to you, you will weep and lament, but the world will rejoice; you will be sorrowful, but your sorrow will turn into joy" [John

16:20]. This does not mean that their sorrow was to be succeeded by joy, but that it was to be transformed into joy, be changed into a higher supernatural joy. So St. Paul could say, "For the sake of Christ I am content (or "I take pleasure in," as the Authorized Version translates) with weaknesses, insults, hardships, persecutions, and calamities; for when I am weak, then I am strong" [2 Corinthians 12:10]. Bearing these things for Christ's sake, he is content. His sorrow is turned into joy.

But suffering with and for Christ has a much deeper meaning. It leads to actual union with the crucified. It enables us in some real sense to share in his redemptive work. So lovers of Jesus have spoken of the "joyful vocation to suffering." We are allowed to share in our Lord's passion. We share in his passion by the fact that, as members of his mystical body, Jesus himself suffers in us and with us. This is the strange truth contained in those mysterious words of St. Paul, "Now I rejoice in my sufferings for your sake, and in my flesh I complete what is lacking in Christ's afflictions for the sake of his body, that is, the Church" [Colossians 1:24].

AVOIDING PAIN

The attempt to avoid pain at any cost and in every possible way has led to frightful evils in the world. In this "fallen" world, only the acceptance of pain can retrieve the balance and restore our understanding of reality. Because they understood this, the saints became what they were. To understand this is to grasp the secret of the saints.

So our Lord steadfastly set his face to go to Jerusalem, there to suffer and there to die [Luke 9:51]. Peter, the chief of the apostles, Peter who had just been commended by Jesus for his faith, tried to dissuade him, "God forbid, Lord! This shall never happen to you" [Matthew 16:22]. To Peter the cross seemed entirely unnecessary. So some of us think of the cross as entirely unnecessary in our lives, and not a few, nowadays, try to remove the cross from the Christian religion.

Why did Jesus set his face to go to Jerusalem? Why did he not turn back and follow the easier way: back to his home in Nazareth, back to his mother and his friends, where he could have settled down happily, and where he could have continued his teaching in peace? Where he could have escaped the cross? Why not? Because man's rejection of the Father's gift of his Son made it necessary that the Son "should endure the cross, despising the shame" [Hebrews 12:2]. Because the cross was the only way in which a sinful world could be saved.

So Satan, himself, through Peter, would try to suggest to Jesus the avoidance of the cross. That was why our Lord said to Peter, "Get behind me. Satan! You are a hindrance to me; for you are not on the side of God, but of men" [Matthew 16:23]. Satan will suggest to us also, often, how desirable it will be to avoid the cross, and easy ways of doing so.

It is then essential, if we would follow Christ, to take up the cross. We are not merely to accept it grudgingly as an unavoidable burden. We are to "take it up." We are to accept it trustingly and lovingly. Only by willingly accepting the cross can it become a source of redemption and a blessing to us. Sometimes, as we have been thinking, it is possible for us to refuse or escape the cross. There are other times when the cross will come into our lives whether we like it or not. Shall I take up the cross or shall I let it lay me low? Let us try, with God's help, to accept the cross willingly and joyfully, for this is to accept our Christian vocation to suffer along with Jesus.

"I have been crucified with Christ; it is no longer I who live, but Christ who lives in me; and the life I now live in the flesh I live by faith in the Son of God, who loved me and gave himself for me" [Galatians 2:20].

This then is our vocation, to take up our cross and follow Jesus, in trustful love that we shall share in the hidden joy that he himself found in the acceptance of the Holy Cross. "Who for the joy that was set before him endured the cross, despising the shame, and is seated at the right hand of the throne of God" [Hebrews 12:2].

### The Crown

*1 Peter 5:4   And when the chief Shepherd is manifested you will obtain the unfading crown of glory.*

We have been thinking of the difficulties which are a necessary part of our vocation as Christians. We must also remember that we must be ever looking beyond and above those things and must rest in the heavenly hope which, in a real sense, is ours already. "For this slight momentary affliction is preparing for us an eternal weight of glory beyond all comparison, because we look not to the things that are seen but to the things that are unseen; for the things that are seen are transient, but the things that are unseen are eternal" [2 Corinthians 4:17–18].

The Psalmist tells us, "For ever, O Lord, is thy word firmly fixed in the heavens" [Psalm 119:89].

The Word of God abides eternally with the Father in heaven. We can take this, not as referring only to the Eternal Word dwelling in the bosom of the Father but also to the Incarnate Word, Jesus the Word made flesh, now glorified and seated at the right hand of the Father. "Jesus Christ is the same yesterday and today and forever" [Hebrews 13:8]. Having once assumed our manhood, the Word of God will never put it aside. In his ascension our Lord carried our humanity to the right hand of the throne of God. "I am ascending to my Father and your Father, to my God and your God" [John 20:17]. The words seem to indicate that, in some true spiritual sense, our Lord carries us up with him to the right hand of the Father. There in heaven he exercises his eternal priesthood, pleading for us in and through that body which he took of blessed Mary. There he pleads for us, as here on earth we plead his passion at our altars by means of his sacramental body.

GOD'S PURPOSE FOR US

There in heaven, too, he makes ready to welcome each of us to our eternal home. There he makes ready for us our eternal glory. "in my Father's house are many rooms; if it were not so, would I have told you that I go to prepare a place for you? And when I go and prepare a place for you, I will come again and take you to myself, that where I am you may be also" [John 14:2-3].

God's purpose for us is that our humanity may be glorified, in and through the humanity of Jesus Christ. "Thou hast made him [man] little less than God, and dost crown him with glory and honor" [Psalm 8:5]. God's ultimate plan for us was that we should "be crowned with glory and honor." That glorification had been accomplished in the humanity of Christ. Our common humanity, assumed by Christ and shared by Christ, now reigns on the throne of the universe. Since our humanity has thus been exalted in him, we need to venerate that humanity made sacred in him. How we ought, for this reason, to reverence our bodies in every way; to rejoice in the wonder of man's works; to glory in the high hopes and good aspirations of mankind.

CHRISTIANITY AND HUMANISM

The true Christian must be a true humanist: we cannot hold that the end of man is to sink down into dust and ashes, but to be crowned with glory and honor, along with Jesus Christ. "God has shown me," said St. Peter in Acts, "that I should not call any man common or unclean" [Acts 10:28]. We must not despise or look down on any of our fellow men or women. We must not despise the body or neglect its proper care and its proper needs.

We do need to practice a measure of self-discipline and self-denial because of our "fallen" condition, but the purpose of such discipline is not to injure or destroy the body, but to prepare it to be a better instrument of the spirit. St. Francis of Assisi, after a life of great asceticism, was led to confess that he had been "too hard on Brother Ass," as he called his body.

"From [heaven] . . . we await a Savior, the Lord Jesus Christ, who will change our lowly body to be like his glorious body, by the power which enables him even to subject all things to himself" [Philippians 3:20–21]. We cannot set any limits to the possibilities of what God can work in us if we will let him. "We know that when he appears we shall be like him. . . . And everyone who thus hopes in him purifies himself as he is pure" [1 John 3:2–3].

Think, too, of the wonderful power of Christ's heavenly intercession. In heaven, the atoning power of Jesus' sacrifice is continually pleaded for us, by his very presence there. Our great high priest, "is able for all

time to save those who draw near to God through him, since he always lives to make intercession for them" [Hebrews 7:25]. As Father Benson has said, "He was going to the Father, not to lay aside the office in which he had cared for us on earth, but to exercise that office in a heavenly manner, being exalted to the right hand of power."

OUR TRUE NATIVE LAND

It is this heavenly intercession of Jesus Christ which makes effective and powerful our earthly intercessions because our earthly intercessions are united with his. "Whatever you ask in my name, I will do it, that the Father may be glorified in the Son; if you ask anything in my name, I will do it" [John 14:13–14]. To ask in Christ's name is to ask as identified with Christ. It is to pray the prayer of Christ himself, to join in the heavenly intercession of Christ.

Our little prayers seem to us feeble and earthbound: but, inasfar as they are made in Christ's name and Spirit, they become truly heavenly prayers and are re-presented to the Father through the lips of our great high priest in heaven, just as our altars which seem to stand on earth are really one with the heavenly altar on which stands the sacrificial Lamb. What a wonderful power we have in prayer, and how great is our privilege to share in it. Our hopes and prayers are sure to be fulfilled and answered since Christ always lives to make intercession for us.

Here and now we have already entered into the resurrection life, the ascended life, the glorified life. "Our commonwealth is in heaven" [Philippians 3:20]. That is our true dwelling place, our true home, and you and I are called upon to live day by day in the power of that heavenly life. The little acts of love that we are doing here are lifting us up from earth to heaven. Every effort made for God, every heartfelt prayer, every kindness done to our neighbor, comes from God "the Father of lights" [James 1:17] and so returns to him. All good deeds are laid up safe in heaven; these are those heavenly treasures which our Lord bids us to lay up for ourselves [Matthew 6:20]. Let us begin now to furnish that heavenly mansion which Jesus has prepared for us. Let us prepare now to live there in our true heavenly home.

If then you have been raised with Christ, seek the things that are above, where Christ is, seated at the right hand of God. Set your minds on things that are above, not on things that are on earth.                    [Colossians 3:1-2].

Chapter 5

ETERNITY AND TIME

*"Life," a cynic has said,*

*"is a long preparation*

*for something that never happens."*

Eternity

*Revelation 1:8 " 'I am the Alpha and the Omega,' says the Lord God, who is and who was and who is to come, the Almighty."*

We are living nowadays in a period of great and rapid change. We are very conscious of the transitoriness of all created things and of the uncertainties of the future which lie before us. So it is good and necessary to remind ourselves that, in contrast to the passing and changing

things on earth, God is eternal. The words chosen for our text are a kind of summary of the spiritual meaning of the whole book of Revelation.

In that book, the seer undertakes to write in type and symbol the whole future history of the world. As we read its pages, what do we find? Many things that are both disturbing and perplexing—wars, tumults, terrors, plagues, troubles, the testings and tribulations of the saints. This, in type and symbol, is history—history as it has been in the past, history as it now is, history as it shall be to the end of time.

### CHANGES WITHIN THE UNCHANGING

The point of the book is this: All these foretold troubles and uncertainties and judgments are not to bring fear, terror, or despair to those who hold fast to Jesus Christ. In Christ, we are safe and secure. Behind all these changes, eternal love abides. God is both the Alpha and the Omega: he is the first and also the last of the letters of the Greek alphabet. He is the beginning and the end, yes and the middle too. He spans all time. Indeed he is greater than time because he abides eternally, ruling and directing all things in accordance with his own holy and loving purposes.

This thought of the eternity of God is stressed over and over again in this book of Revelation. In the first chapter, this thought is repeated no less than three times. In verse 4, the salutation reads, "Grace to you and peace from him who is and who was and who is to come." In verse 8, as we have seen, God declares, "I am the Alpha and the Omega." The glorified Christ proclaims in verse 17, "Fear not, I am the first and the last." At the end of the book, just before the unveil-

ing of the glories of the heavenly Jerusalem, the same assurance is given, "It is done! I am the Alpha and the Omega, the beginning and the end" [Revelation 21:6].

So, in the midst of many uncertainties, we must look with gratitude and perfect love and hope and trust to our God, the eternal one—or, rather, the eternal three-in-one—whose blessed name, Father, Son, and Holy Spirit, speaks to us of perfect and eternal love. Our God is not a lonely, loveless unity, but a unity of love. The Father eternally loves the Son; the Son in turn, eternally loves the Father; and this very love of God, being himself eternal Spirit, proceeds from the Father to the Son, and from the Son to the Father. And that divine love is so great, so vast, so unconfined that it passes out, as it were, beyond itself. Love creates a universe with the signature of love stamped all over it for those who have eyes to see.

Then, when sin had entered in and spoiled things, love made a further leap. Eternal love became incarnate in the Babe of Bethlehem, and the divine love, beyond all human thought, is revealed to us through the human love of the holy heart of Jesus. Our humanity, made one with God through the incarnation, becomes an abiding factor within the Godhead. The human Jesus is one with the eternal Word of God; and Christ Jesus, glorified in heaven, has passed beyond the limits of our changing and temporal mortality so that it can be written of him, "Jesus Christ is the same yesterday and today and for ever" [Hebrews 13:8]. He too is the Alpha and the Omega, who is and who was and who is to come.

As we look back over our lives, we shall experience inevitably some sorrow and regret. There are the many lost opportunities, our frequent failures to respond to God's grace, the many occasions when, yielding to temptation, we have fallen into sin. Then too we mourn the loss of beloved friends and others dear to us, taken from us by the passage of time, no longer with us here on earth. But we must go on to remember also, to our great and endless comfort, that everything that is truly lovely, desirable, and beautiful, all that we have "loved and lost awhile," still abides in God himself, who is altogether lovely. And in him too the past is purified. Our past failures and sins and mistakes and imperfections all are swallowed up in his victorious love. They are burned up in the consuming fire of the divine

charity. Only the pure gold will remain.

### THE UNHAPPINESS IN CHILDHOOD

All of us have known times when we looked back with nostalgic longing to our "happy childhood." A little thought, however, will convince us that our childhood was not really as happy as we like to think. After all, there were a good many tears in childhood, a good many pains and sorrows and disappointments that were indeed very terrible when we had to face them. Now most of these unhappinesses are forgotten, and only the happy memories remain. Something like this is the way that we shall see things when we come to be with God in heaven. God abides, and God is good, and God is pure, and God is love. In that abiding love we are safe. In that abiding love is our true happiness.

Already, in a very true sense, we have been raised above the weakness and change of our fallen humanity by the gift of new life which Jesus came to bring to us. We have already been born anew, born from above, of water and the Spirit. Even now we have entered into the heavenly kingdom. We are members of Christ, parts of the Body of Christ. We are the children of God and inheritors of the eternal kingdom. So he reminds each one of us individually, "I am the Alpha": I am the beginning, *your* beginning. Out of nothingness, God brought me into my life here on earth. Even before my natural birth, before my conception, eternal God, eternal Love intended me to be his child. Having given me the gift of natural life, he added to that the supreme gift of supernatural life.

"But when the goodness and loving kindness of God our Savior appeared, he saved us, not because of deeds done by us in righteousness, but in virtue of his own mercy, by washing of regeneration and renewal in the Holy Spirit, which he poured out upon us richly through Jesus Christ our Savior, so that we might be justified by his grace and become heirs in hope of eternal life. The saying is sure" [Titus 3:4-8].

### THE PRIZE

So we must put away all base fears, all wrong sorrows, and make a great act of faith and hope in the transforming power of the eternal love revealed in Jesus Christ. We must look forward to the goal, as St. Paul tells us to do. "One thing I do, forgetting what lies behind and straining forward to what lies ahead, I press on toward the goal for the prize of the upward call of God in Christ Jesus" [Philippians 3:13-14].

The prize is truly a supernatural prize. Do not let us be satisfied with anything less than this. Do not let us aim too low. The purpose and end of merely natural man is perfectly to fulfill his humanity. He or she is called upon to rise up to the full ideals possible to humanity: to become a great, a noble man or woman. Only a very few can attain to this ideal; and, when all is done, as our poets and dramatists and novelists remind us, death ends all. "Life," a cynic has said, "is a long preparation for something that never happens." Death ends all.

For the Christian, however, death is but the beginning of real life. God is the Alpha, but God is also the Omega, and death is not the end.

As Christians we are called to rise up to something greater than the perfection of our natural humanity. We are called upon to attain to the measure of the fullness of the stature of Christ, and Christ is the victor over death and hell. For God has "called us to his own glory and excellence, by which he has granted to us his precious and very great promises, that through these you may escape from the corruption that is in the world . . . and become

partakers of the divine nature"
[2 Peter 1:3-4].

"I am the Alpha and the
Omega," and every letter of the
alphabet in between! I am the
beginning and the end and the
middle and the now. As day
succeeds day in our pilgrimage
here on earth, we must always
remember the promise of Jesus,
"Lo, I am with you always, to
the close of the age" [Matthew
28:20].

### Time

*O God, our help in ages past,*
  *Our hope for years to come,*
*Our shelter from the stormy*
      *blast,*
*And our eternal home.*

                  *   *   *

*Time, like an ever-rolling stream,*
  *Bears all its sons away;*
*They fly, forgotten, as a dream*
  *Dies at the opening day.*
                  *[Isaac Watts*
    *Hymn 289, after Psalm 90]*

Time is indeed "like an ever-
rolling stream." The characteristic of time, as we know it, is its
endless flow. It is like a river.
We cannot stop it. We cannot
even wade into the same river,
for the water that was there a
moment ago has flowed away.

Past, present, future—so we
speak of time. Yet we directly
experience only the present, and
how strange the notion of the
present is! It is like a knife

blade, infinitely narrow, dividing
the past, stored in the memory,
from the unknown future, which
we grasp only in imagination,
anticipation, or hope.

### WHAT IS REAL?

The present, we say, is *real.* It
is here and now. Yet, how real is
the present? Can I ever know it?
As soon as I seek to grasp it or
even think about it, it is already
past, already gone, already over.
Even the present, I can "have"
only in my memory.

So our life in time is like a
series of momentary flitting
pictures, something like a motion
picture film. The pictures we see
on the screen are not alive and
do not themselves move. They
come to life and movement only
because a human spectator sees
them on the screen and in some
mysterious way stores them in
his memory.

So I experience life, the world
of time and change, and hold the
past in memory and the future in
anticipation only because I live—
only because I exist. My eyes,
my senses, my brain have their
part in building up and creating
the world I live in. All this is
possible only because I exist, and
go on existing, and bind all these
passing and changing things into
one.

Now this is a very profound
and important thing when we
begin to think about it. In the

Old Testament, in the scene in the desert when the Almighty reveals himself to Moses in the burning bush, he announced his name as "I AM WHO I AM." In a certain true sense, you and I also can say, "I am." Because we can say that, you and I can know the world and time and life. My *derived* existence is somehow bound up with the eternal existence of almighty God, and this derived and dependent existence makes it possible for me to have fellowship with the eternal God who is absolute existence and perfect life. I, in my derived creaturely existence, can have fellowship with the eternal Father, who is eternal life and eternal love.

As I gaze into the mirror of memory and see the past, I behold there a mixture of goodness and evil. Because of this, I look into the future with a mixture of hope and fear. As we said earlier, we can trust the love and the almighty power of God to redeem and purify the past. The almighty power of God can forgive our sins, blot out our transgressions, and bring good out of evil just as he brought redemption out of the awful cross on Calvary. So too, we must by faith make an act of complete trust in God for the future and believe that our spiritual hopes will be justified and our fears proved false. Why not? God is

the great I AM. In him alone all time is the eternal present. In the reality of his Being, he has no fading memories of the past or uncertain hopes of the future, but he sees the whole at once. For him, the stream no longer moves. He is at the center of all things. So my highest hopes for the future and my purest desires for the future are not hopes or desires in him; but are *even now* actual, real, true, present. So if I put my hopes in him, I shall not be disappointed. "Let me not be disappointed of my hope," the Psalmist prays [Psalm 119:116].

## FUTURE TRIALS AND HOPE

We cannot then be disappointed in the realization of our spiritual hopes if we put our faith and trust in the eternal Father. We are thinking here of spiritual hopes, not of mere natural human desires. The security of our spiritual hope does not mean, of course, that there will be no difficulties or trials or temptations in the future.

We have been thinking about the book of Revelation and trying to discover something of its inner meaning in the light of the words, "I am the Alpha and the Omega." Most of that book is filled with terrible happenings, frightful trials and difficulties. Even the souls of the righteous ones, "who had been slain for the word of God and for the witness they had borne; they cried out with a loud voice, '. . . How long?' " [Revelation 6:9-10]. They are still under the tyranny of time. All of us have to undergo this discipline of waiting in patient hope. Our Lord has reminded us, "A disciple is not above his teacher, nor a servant above his master" [Matthew 10:24]. The followers of Jesus must be prepared to follow him along the long and painful way of the cross. But the way of the cross is also the way of triumph. Our Lord will enable us to persevere through every difficulty. "My grace is sufficient for you" [2 Corinthians 12:9].

Let us then, as we think of these things, resolve to "lay aside every weight, and the sin which clings so closely, and let us run with perseverance the race that is set before us, looking to Jesus the pioneer and perfecter of our faith" [Hebrews 12:1-2] —Jesus our Alpha and our Omega.

With the sure help of the eternity of God, then, I shall be enabled to live my difficult life in time. Concerning the blessed ones in the heavenly kingdom, it is written that they "follow the Lamb wherever he goes" [Revelation 14:4]. That is our vocation, too, here on earth, simply to follow Jesus, the Lamb, wherever he may lead us. We are to follow him as readily through the valley of the shadow of death as when he brings us into green pastures or leads us alongside the still waters. We know that, since he is leading us, it is safer and better always to be where he is than in any other place. Some place of our own choosing may seem to us to be safer and better, but it is never better than the place where he leads us, even if that place be the valley of the shadow of death. We must simply follow the Lamb, "wherever he goes."

Finding, following, keeping, struggling,
  Is he sure to bless?
Angels, Martyrs, Prophets, Virgins,
  Answer, "Yes!"
        [John Mason Neale
        English Hymnal, 366]

TIME AND DEATH

In Christ Jesus, we have already passed from death into life. In the creed we say, "I look for the Resurrection of the dead; And the Life of the world to come." In a very real sense, however, the life of that world to come—eternal life—is already ours. So Jesus said to Martha at the grave of Lazarus, "Whoever lives and believes in me shall never die" [John 11:26]. Our life, our true life, as the Apostle reminds us, "is hid with Christ in God" [Colossians 3:3]. The Christian life is life in Christ—life in God. As we follow Christ, we live in Christ; our life becomes transformed into his life. By the power of the Holy Spirit, the eternal, the true, the resurrection life in Christ is even now being built up within our mortal bodies. "Whoever lives and believes in me shall never die."

Thus the problem of living under the weight of time is solved for us. Outward difficulties, bodily weaknesses, aches and pains, diseases cannot really overcome us. "So we do not lose heart. Though our outer nature is wasting away, our inner nature is being renewed every day. For this slight momentary affliction is preparing for us an eternal weight of glory beyond all comparison, because we look not to the things that are seen but to the things that are unseen; for the things that are seen are transient, but the things that are unseen are eternal" [2 Corinthians 4:16–18]. The things that are seen are the things of time. Even while we behold them, they change and pass away. But the unseen realities, grasped by faith, abide forever in the life and love of the eternal, almighty God.

"I am the Alpha and the Omega." The book of Revelation ends with the same thought with which it began. " 'Behold, I am coming soon, bringing my recompense, to repay every one for what he has done. I am the Alpha and the Omega, the first and the last, the beginning and the end. . . . I Jesus . . . am the root and the offspring of David, the bright morning star.' The Spirit and the Bride say, 'Come.' And let him who hears say, 'Come.' And let him who is thirsty come, let him who desires take the water of life without price. . . . He who testifies to these things says, 'Surely I am coming soon.' Amen. Come Lord Jesus!" And Jesus was already with him, and the life of Jesus was already his.

Chapter 6

## CHARITY OR CHRISTIAN LOVE

*There are ways of speaking the truth
which only
drive people away from the truth.*

### Love is Patient and Kind

Let us think of the character of love as St. Paul sets it before us. As we go on, we shall find that in this virtue of love are included practically all the virtues that we need for our Christian lives.

*1 Corinthians 13:4   Love is patient and kind.*

Here are the basic negative and positive characteristics of the virtue of charity. Love is patient, long suffering, slow to anger, slow in showing annoyance, ready to bear disappoint-

46

ment and loss, ready to endure grief and pain. This is the negative side of the virtue of love.

On the positive side, love is kind, truly sympathetic, on the watch for opportunities of doing good and making others happy; love is tolerant and forgiving, trying as far as may be to put oneself in the other person's place.

The word "patience," as you know, comes from a Latin root which means "to suffer." We learn patience by suffering or enduring difficult, painful, and unpleasant things. The Epistle of St. James counsels us, "Let every man be quick to hear, slow to speak, slow to anger, for the anger of man does not work the righteousness of God" [James 1:19–20].

The anger of man has never worked the righteousness of God and never will. Yet we think that somehow or other it will do so! Think of our Lord's great patience with the apostles, with their stupidity, their slowness, their dullness of comprehension. Here is love in operation. Again and again he tries gently to teach them, yet they do not comprehend. But his patience is not exhausted, and gradually they learn. He does not allow their dullness and stupidity to get on his nerves, as we say. If we are to love as we are bidden to love, we must not let dullness or stupidity get on our nerves either.

### RIGHTEOUS INDIGNATION

We are very like our Lord's disciples—very unlike our Lord. We are quite sure that the wrath of man *can* work the righteousness of God. Whenever we get angry, we are quite sure that this is a case of righteous indignation. That is a blanket excuse for all our fits of anger. Peter drew his sword and cut off the ear of the servant of the high priest, who had come with the mob to the garden to arrest Jesus. Surely Peter was moved by righteous indignation, if there ever was such. But Jesus rebuked Peter and healed the ear of the servant [Luke 22:48–51].

We too are all for hacking our way through. We are all for finding some easy short cut. We are so unready to go on in the patient endurance which love demands. We must develop the sort of zeal which patiently suffers for the truth's sake, the only kind of zeal which ever converted anyone. We can convert people to love of our Lord only by showing them the supernatural endurance which love alone gives.

Then love is patient in bearing disappointment and hardships and griefs, with a smile on the lips and gladness in the heart in spite of sorrow. When the call to suffering comes, love delights to suffer with its Master, Christ.

Henry Suso, the 14th century German mystic, tells us of a time in his life when he was crossing Lake Constance in a little boat. He had as his companion a magnificent knight, dressed in a suit of shining armor. They fell into conversation, and Suso was much impressed by the knight's account of the tournaments in which he took part, of the hardness of the combats they had to endure, of the wounds they had to suffer —all for the sake of the ring which they hoped to win as their prize. The knight went on to remark that, even when wounded in these combats, they paid no attention to their wounds.

"May not one weep to show one is hurt when one is hit very hard?" asked Suso, who was greatly astonished.

"No," the knight replied. "No, even though one's heart fails, one must never show that he is distressed. One must appear gay and happy. Otherwise he is dishonored and loses both his reputation and the ring."

Suso tells us that he was greatly moved by these words.

"O Lord," he said, inwardly sighing, "if the knights of this world must suffer so much to obtain so small a prize, how just it is that we should suffer far more if we are to obtain an eternal recompense. O my sweet Lord, if only I were worthy of being thy spiritual knight!"

Besides being patient, love is also kind. As far as may be, love is always ready to give itself to the service of others. In our Lord's parable of the good Samaritan [Luke 10], we are told that the poor wounded traveler was lying by the side of the road. The priest and the Levite, both of them clerics, whose very calling, one would think, would have impelled them to show compassion and give help, "passed by on the other side." They were too busy with other, more important, things. They did not want to get involved with something which would demand time and trouble.

Then the Samaritan, representing love in its kindness, comes along. When he saw that poor man, "he had compassion." He looked after him, bound up his wounds, made provision for care for him in his distress. Nowadays it would be unlikely that any of us would behave in such an unfeeling and selfish way as did the priest and the Levite. We would feel ashamed to do so. Our own reputation, should our conduct be known, would suffer.

We are forced by public opinion and our own self-respect to show outward kindnesses in cases of manifest outward need of assistance, like the instance in the parable.

### TODAY'S WOUNDED PEOPLE

Unfortunately, however, there are many other instances in which we fail to show kindness to others. Very often there are all around us—sometimes very close to us—men and women who are wounded and need help, wounded not physically but spiritually, half dead with sorrow or worry, half dead with loneliness or fear because they have no one in whom they can confide. All around us every day there are people who are crying out for just the smallest bit of human sympathy, the smallest deed of human kindness, the kind word or the smile. Such little signs of interest or concern, such smallest pledges of love, can often work a miracle and save a brother from sadness and despair.

We excuse ourselves from the effort of trying to be kind to others by saying to ourselves that these griefs and troubles are imaginary and perhaps "ought not to be encouraged." Very likely the troubles are often imaginary, but what of that? Loving sympathy goes out to enter into the point of view of our sad and sorrowing and lonely neighbor. A child weeping over a broken doll is imagining a loss far beyond the reality, and in a short time the doll will be completely forgotten. At the time, the sorrow and the loss are very real.

In God's sight, we too are children, often weeping over what are merely broken toys. When we get to heaven it may well be that we shall laugh over things that now seem most grievous. But the griefs are real to us now, and supposed imaginary griefs are real to other people. Love demands that we try to look at these trials from their standpoint, rather than from ours.

Let us pray for grace to be more kind, more really sympathetic, more compassionate. Many of us who are naturally reserved must make a real effort, by God's help, to show love and kindness and sympathy to others. If our hearts are cold, if we do not *feel* interest or compassion or affection for others, let us force ourselves, as it were, to go through the motions of love. Then, perhaps, God in his grace will give us an increase of real love. "Bear one another's burdens, and so fulfill the law of Christ" [Galatians 6:2]. We will be given the strength and the courage to bear the sorrows of many people, which they cannot bear themselves. We can help to tide them through present difficulties. We can assist them to keep going. When we are doing this, God will give us others to help us likewise in our times of need. Love showing itself in deeds of kindness is Christianity in action. This is the love of Christ himself becoming reincarnate in the hearts of other men and women.

"There is an idea among most people," said Robert Louis Stevenson, "that they should make their neighbors good. One person I have to make good—myself. But my duty to my neighbor is much more nearly expressed by saying that I have to make him happy if I may."

## The Humility of Love

*1 Corinthians 13:4    Love is not jealous or boastful.*

Or, in a paraphrase, "Love knows no hatred or envy. It is never braggart in mien or swollen with self-adulation." These things are all manifestations of the sin of pride. The humility of love makes them impossible. Love is not jealous or envious. These are truly dreadful qualities, closely related to each other, but not quite the same. Jealousy is the dislike of sharing with anoth-

er a loved possession. Since jealousy is thus associated with love and affection, we may be led to think that it is almost a necessary part of love, but this is not so.

We are apt to think that jealousy is a part of love because of the several meanings that are attached to our English word "love." "Love" may mean a desire to seize and appropriate something in order to attain to self-satisfaction. Love, in this case, may come to mean pure *selfishness.* The kind of love that St. Paul is commending to us, the divine virtue of love, is rather *selflessness.* Love seeks the happiness and joy of others, rather than the happiness and joy of self. The love that can suffer jealousy is not self-sacrificing, but selfish and self-appropriating.

### HOW LOVE GROWS

A wonderful thing about real love is that the more it is shared, the greater it grows. In this it differs from all material goods. A man tends to cling to his material possessions because he knows that he cannot share them with others without becoming poorer himself. But a generous love is prodigal of sharing material things. The generous love of Mary of Bethany caused her to use the whole "pound of costly

ointment of pure nard" to
anoint the feet of Jesus [John
12:3]. She did not count the
cost. She did not sensibly consider that she need use only
some of the ointment for anoint-
ing and keep the rest. No, her
love wanted to give all. Having
poured out this precious ointment, it was gone. She had lost
possession of it forever. This is
true of all material possessions,
and this is true of all lesser loves
also. Lesser loves become diminished by being shared with
others, but real love can never be
diminished by being shared.
Real love grows in the sharing.
The love of Christ "which surpasses knowledge" [Ephesians
3:19] and which embraces in its
scope all mankind, comes to
each beloved individual not one
whit diminished because it is
shared with others. Love is the
only thing that grows by sharing.
Love gives to the limit and finds
glory in the giving. Love knows
no jealousy.

And love knows no envy.
Envy differs from jealousy in
consisting of dislike of seeing
another person having what we
cannot have ourselves. Therefore envy is worse than jealousy.
There is perhaps some excuse for
jealousy, since it fears the loss of
a loved possession, but envy
hates to see another possess what
it never had itself and what it

never can have. We are not im-
poverished at all by the fact that
someone else has something of
value which we do not and cannot have. Nevertheless we
resent the fact that the other
person has it. Envy is the attitude of the dog in the manger in
the old story, who, unable to eat
the fodder of the cattle, nevertheless prevents the cattle from
having their food. Love knows
no envy.

Followers of Christ need to be
on their guard against a kind of
spiritual envy—envy of those
who seem to be able to pray
better than we can, envy of
people who are obviously better
Christians than we are. To desire
good gifts is right. To envy
others who have them is wrong.

THE PLACE OF HONOR

Envy, like jealousy, arises from
pride. So St. Paul goes on at
once to remind us that love is
not boastful. Love, in its good
works, does not wish to be seen
of men. "Beware of practicing
your piety before men," says our
Lord in his Sermon on the
Mount. "When you give alms,
sound no trumpet before you.
When you give alms, do not
let your left hand know what
your right hand is doing" [Matt-
hew 6:1-3].

Nor does love seek out "the
places of honor at feasts and the

best seats in the synagogues, and salutations in the market places" [Matthew 23:6-7]. Love does not seek out the front pages of the newspapers and the flattering publicity which are so generally sought for nowadays. Love makes no parade.

Jesus Christ, the God incarnate, Savior of the world, was content for thirty years to live and work, unadvertised and unknown, in a small obscure village. Father Benson has reminded us that, "the divine hiddenness is always far more enduring than human display."

The remedy for jealousy and the remedy for boastfulness is humility, and humility is part of true love. Perfect humility is free from any possible humiliation. He who subjects himself to his neighbor in love, says St. Basil, can never be humiliated. Humility rejoices in the material or spiritual blessings of another, being itself content to remain in the lowest place. "Let the greatest among you become as the youngest, and the leader as one who serves. For which is the greater, one who sits at table, or one who serves? . . . But I am among you as one who serves" [Luke 22:26-27].

Let us look at our Lord Jesus as the supreme example of humility. Let us see him, as a baby, lying in the cold and poverty of the manger; let us see him in the humble home and in the wearisome tasks of Nazareth; let us see him stretched out naked on the cross, deserted by his friends, while terrible darkness overwhelms his soul; and let us remember that he who has so little is God incarnate and that he willed to have it so. "He who humbles himself will be exalted" [Luke 14:11].

In the Epistle to the Philippians, St. Paul points to the example of our Lord's incarnation as a call to all of us to grow in humility. "Have this mind among yourselves, which you have in Christ Jesus, who, though he was in the form of God, did not count equality with God a thing to be grasped, but emptied himself, taking the form of a servant, being born in the likeness of man" [Philippians 2:5-7]. Would I be willing to be a servant even to the best of men? Yet Jesus Christ, for us men and our salvation, was not unwilling to become the servant of all men.

THE GENTLENESS
OF LOVE

Love "is not arrogant or rude. Love does not insist on its own way; it is not irritable or resentful" [1 Corinthians 13:5]. Love is gentle, in that old-fashioned sense of the word in which we used to speak of a gentleman or a gentlewoman.

Love is courteous. It does not offend good feeling or insist on all it has claim to. Politeness has been well defined as love in trifles. Love will not knowingly and purposely do things which, perhaps quite harmless in themselves, unnecessarily offend others. Sometimes, of course, though perhaps not often, it may be necessary to offend others in the interests of truth.

Love possesses that elusive gift that we call tact, a very difficult thing for us to acquire and to use. Love sees things so completely from the other person's point of view that it knows exactly the right and proper thing to say or do. Think of the gentleness and tact shown in our Lord's dealings with the woman whom he met at the well in Samaria [John 4]. The woman who came to the well that day to draw water was not one who would be called "a good woman" and Jesus knew this. But he did not begin his conversation with her by reminding her of that fact. Instead, he asked her to do a kindness for him.

"Give me a drink," he said to her. Then, when she begins to talk to him, he says nothing more about his thirst, but he speaks to her so tactfully, so wonderfully, about divine and heavenly things that her conscience, perhaps long dead, awakens, and she confesses her sin.

## SPEAKING THE TRUTH

How much we can learn about the way of dealing with others by meditating on our Lord's dealing with this woman of Samaria! We are, of course, called upon to speak the truth. This, of course, is a duty. But we have to do something much harder than the mere speaking of the truth. We must be careful to speak the truth "in love" [Ephesians 4:15]. There are ways of speaking the truth which only drive people away from the truth.

Some Christians seem to think that it is necessary to prove their zeal and orthodoxy by being as disagreeable and contentious as possible to all others who do not hold to their own opinions. "Love is not arrogant or rude," says St. Paul.

## OUR RIGHTS AND PRIVILEGES

Nor does love "insist on its own way." It does not take advantage of its privileges, nor does it always insist on its rights. It knows that love is more important than rights and privileges. Perhaps this is the truth that lies behind our Lord's difficult saying in the Sermon on the Mount, "If any one would sue you and take your coat, let him have your cloak as well" [Matthew 5:40]. In the same way, St. Paul in discussing the problem of eating food that been offered to idols points out that this is in itself harmless since "an idol has no real existence."

St. Paul then recognizes the fact that this may be "a stumbling block [a scandal] to the weak. . . . Therefore, if food is a cause of my brother's falling, I will never eat meat, lest I cause my brother to fall" [1 Corinthians 8:9, 13]. Love may prevent my doing things which I have a perfect right to do, and in which is no sin, because these things may drive my brother or sister away from our Lord, Jesus Christ.

Love is not irritable or resentful. It is not seeking opportunities to find fault or to start a quarrel. Such opportunities, of course, can be quite easily found if we go around looking for them. Love is not quick to take offence. It is not easily provoked. The Greek word used here is the basis of our English word "paroxysm." Love does not give way to fits of rage. The same word is used in the 15th chapter of Acts to describe the heated quarrel between Paul and Barnabas. The contention between them was so sharp that they separated from each other [Acts 15:39]. This particular quarrel will shed a good deal of light upon the foolish character of many of our quarrels. For this was a quarrel between two men who were later canonized saints concerning the good character of a third canonized saint!

Love stores up no resentment. There is a harmful form of "mental bookkeeping" in which many indulge. It consists of storing up in our memories a complete list of all the wrongs and injuries that we have had to suffer from someone else in the hope of "getting even" some day. Love is not mindful of past wrongs. It forgives and forgets.

"I can forgive, but I can't forget," we hear people say. That, of course, means that the person using such words has not really forgiven at all. Let it all go, as God lets it go.

"I will be merciful toward their iniquities, and I will remember their sins no more" [Hebrews 8:12]. Love readily forgives because it knows its own need of forgiveness. God freely forgives me, but on one condition—that I must in turn forgive the wrongs that have been done to me. "For if you forgive men their trespasses, your heavenly Father also will forgive you; but if you do not forgive men their trespasses, neither will your Father forgive your trespasses" [Matthew 6:14-15]. Sometimes it is very hard really to forgive. Yet things that one can forgive easily are hardly worth forgiving. Real forgiveness is difficult forgiveness.

It will help us to forgive others if we learn to try to make excuses for other people, who often look at things very differently from the way we do. So, when the Roman soldiers were nailing our Lord to the cross, his thought seemed to be, "I must find an excuse for them! I must include them in the love of my heart." So he prayed, "Father, forgive them; for they know not what they do" [Luke 23:34]. And that was surely true! These Roman soldiers, from their point of view, were only doing their duty. "They know not what they do." The same excuse applies in some measure, almost always, when others injure us. Very seldom do they fully know, or intend, the injury done to us.

The measure of forgiveness which I may expect from God depends upon the measure of forgiveness which I am giving to those who have injured me. Is my love like that of Jesus Christ? Love stores up no resentment.

## How Love Rejoices

*1 Corinthians 13:6 Love does not rejoice at wrong, but rejoices in the right.*

Love never exults over wrongdoing under any circumstances. No advantage which may accrue to us because of the sin of others can cause love to rejoice in that which ruins the world. Thus, for instance, if someone in an influential position has attacked us or our beliefs and later on makes a moral misstep and is thus reduced to silence, love can never rejoice at this. Love will pray for the conversion of its enemies, never for their downfall through misdoing, and love will not take pleasure in hearing tales of the sins and wrongdoing of opponents.

In a famous woodcarving at Nikko in Japan, three monkeys are represented. One has his hands over his eyes, another has his hands over his ears, while the third has his hands over his mouth. The significance of this, we are told, is that we are to see no evil, hear no evil, and speak no evil. The little carving is inspired by Buddhist teaching but is surely consonant with the Christian religion. The monkeys' lesson is a Christian lesson—that we must beware of detraction and gossip. The third chapter of the Epistle of St. James has much to say about the evils that arise from sins of the tongue. "No human being can tame the tongue—a restless evil, full of deadly poison" [James 3:8]. But God can subdue our tongues, if we look to him and ask his help.

THE SINS
OF GOOD PEOPLE

Gossip, detraction, slander, backbiting—these are, alas! often the special sins of those we call "good people." These are the weeds which spring up in the garden of the soul and prevent the blooming of those beautiful flowers which Jesus wants to see there.

St. Bernard tells us that the tongue of the backbiter is a viper which poisons three persons with a single bite; a lance which pierces three men with one thrust; a three-pointed sword which causes three wounds with one blow.

The first wound, he says, is received by him against whom the remark is directed, piercing him to the quick in his good name.

The second wound is received in the mind of the listener, who is scandalized by the remark and who may thereby fall himself into sin.

But the third and worst wound is inflicted in the speaker, piercing his soul with a mortal blow, making it hateful in the eyes of the good and loving God.

Why is it that we so often indulge in this sort of thing? Sometimes gossip arises from our own pride and vanity. We like to have others seek our company, we like to think that our conversation is sparkling and interesting, and, because it is not really sparkling or interesting, we spice our conversation with bits of gossip, bringing in, as a source of abiding interest, the real or imaginary faults and failings and sins of our neighbors.

Before we repeat anything tending to the discredit of others, it would be well to ask ourselves three questions:

Is it true?
Is it kind?
Is it necessary to say it?

As most of our remarks would not pass the test of these questions, the asking of them would greatly limit the scope of our conversation. On the other hand, these questions would save us from many sins. Occasionally it may be really necessary to say something which is disagreeable yet true about our neighbor, but this must be for the sake of kindness, either to the neighbor himself for his own growth in holiness or for the protection of other people. This exception does not occur very often.

Love rejoices in the right. Love rejoices in the truth. It delights in seeing the triumph of the truth, even if, as sometimes happens, the truth is contrary to one's own cherished beliefs and hopes. Love is never afraid of truth. It believes that the truth will triumph and ought to triumph, because it believes that the truth is of God.

We must never fear that knowledge of the truth will damage our Christian religion if we really believe that our religion must be the religion of truth. Love rejoices in every truth, pleasant or unpleasant.

"You will know the truth," said our Lord, "and the truth will make you free" [John 8:32]. Light, we believe, is better than darkness, for we believe that God is light as well as love.

## The Steadfastness of Love

*1 Corinthians 13:7 Love bears all things, believes all things, hopes all things, endures all things.*

Love, in other words, is always eager and anxious to believe the best about our fellow men. It is never cynical or prejudiced. It would always prefer to be too generous in its estimation of another, rather than to be unjustly suspicious. Love tends to be optimistic and therefore cannot share the outlook on life and on mankind which is so prevalent at the present day. It is fatally easy, alas, to persuade ourselves that the cynical view is true and to become a disillusioned pessimist. That is not a permissible attitude for a Christian.

THE ARID PATH

Mark Twain is usually looked upon as a humorist, but some of his writings toward the end of his life were very bitter indeed. Here, for instance, is a description of the meaning of human life, attributed to him:

A myriad of men are born. They labor and sweat and struggle for bread. They squabble and scold and fight. They scramble for little mean advantages over each other. Age creeps upon them, infirmities follow. Those they love are taken from them. At length, ambition is dead, pride is dead, longing for release is in their breast. It comes at last— the only unpoisoned gift earth ever had for them, and they vanish from a world where they were of no consequence. Then another myriad takes their place and copies all they did, and goes along the same profitless road, and vanishes as they vanished to make room for another, and another, and a million more myriads, who follow the same arid path, through the same desert and accomplish what the first myriad and all the other myriads that came after them accomplished—nothing.

Here is a picture of the world and of humanity which cynicism and so-called "realism" and lack of belief in God and in our fellow men can give us.

But our Christian religion of hope and love assures us that this gloomy appraisal is false, that, in spite of sin and failure, there is still nobility in man and that the image of God is still to be seen in him.

> Two men look out through
>     the same bars,
> One sees mud, and another
>     stars.

With the help of love, it is for us to see the stars in human lives around us.

Love is not prejudiced. Love does not attach unchangeable labels to one's neighbor—liar, cheat, heretic. We can put labels on the jars of preserves which we store away in our cupboards, since we know that when we take the jars down—perhaps a year hence—the contents will still agree with the label.

Men and women are not like that. They are changing all the time. They can grow better; they can be converted. Love is tolerant and hopeful and trusts the grace of God to transform the sinner into the saint. We hope that that is what God is doing in us and for us. Why should he not do it for others also? Love is trustful. Love is hopeful. We must be on our guard against prejudices. We must not judge our brother and attempt to label him before we have seen the end of the story.

### THE DIVINE ELEMENT IN MAN

Love is justified in its supernatural hope and trust because of the divine element in man. The incarnation of our Lord revealed the close kinship existing between man and God so that it was possible for God to reveal himself to man through a human life. If there had been no kinship at all between God and man, the incarnation could not have taken place.

Our Lord has lived his life on earth, died on the cross, risen again, and ascended into heaven. Yet in a real sense he continues to live on earth. He lives in and through his Church, his mystical body. He lives in his members upon earth. He manifests his presence in the hearts and lives of his children. We must learn to see and to love Jesus Christ wherever he manifests himself. We must learn to reverence and adore Jesus Christ as he lives in the hearts of Christians, yes, even in sinful Christians. It is all humanity that Christ united to himself in his incarnation. Let us pray that we may see him, may love him, may trust him in the persons and lives of our brethren.

If we practice this love and hope and trust, we shall find that a miracle takes place. Our own love and trust of others, united with the love of Christ, can play its part in changing and redeeming the world we live in. We are permitted to be "fellow workmen for God" [1 Corinthians 3:9]. Working for and with God, we can use God's own power. The transforming power that Christ brought into the world was the power of redeeming love, and my love, in a measure, can be redemptive too.

This is one of the meanings of the mystery of the communion of saints. Our love for our brethren, our trust in them, our hope for them—these are factors in redeeming them. Our love for them, if it is real, helps them to become like Christ. If we are going to label others at all, the label to be put on them—on every man or woman—is "potential saint."

We must not, and dare not, say of any man or woman, "I know that he is no good" or "She is no good." Something like that was, I am sure, what most of the people of Jerusalem thought about a thief who was crucified with two other men one Friday morning. They were quite convinced that the thief was "no good." Did not his punishment prove it? But we know that Jesus said to him, "Truly, I say to you, today you will be with me in Paradise" [Luke 23:43].

The power of redeeming love is no mere fantasy of the pious mind. It is a fact that "the saints" within the mystical body of Christ can actually influence one another, can really play a part in transforming their fellow men and women by labeling them good and trusting them as good and letting their love go on out to them as good. " 'Knowledge' puffs up, but love builds up" [1 Corinthians 8:1]. We can help to build up others by love. Love believes the best. It trusts and is not disappointed of its hope.

May our part, within the body of Christ, be to show forth that transforming power of joy and love which can raise and has raised up the basest of men and made them true saints of God. God's arm is not shortened. God's power does not fail. God still works miracles. And the power by which God still works miracles is the mighty power of love.

### The Eternity of Love

*1 Corinthians 13:8-10, 13*
*Love never ends; as for*
*prophecy, it will pass away;*
*as for tongues, they will cease;*
*as for knowledge, it will pass*
*away. For our knowledge is*
*imperfect and our prophecy is*
*imperfect; but when the perfect*
*comes, the imperfect will pass*
*away. . . . So faith, hope,*
*love abide, these three; but*
*the greatest of these is love.*

Love can never die, since love is from God and shares in the eternity of God. "Beloved, let us love one another; for love is of God, and he who loves is born of God and knows God . . . for God is love" [1 John 4:7-8]. God is love, and therefore love lasts forever. But other lesser things—even good things—will pass away.

Prophecy will pass away; the "gift of tongues"—so valued in the early Church and being redis-covered in our own day—will also vanish; even knowledge itself will "pass away." For all these things are partial and imperfect.

When absolute completeness shall have come, these fragmen-tary and imperfect things will have no further use.

St. Paul does not say that these imperfect gifts are altogether useless *now.* On the contrary, they have their place. They have their function. They have their purpose. But in the eternal life of heaven, in the radiant light of truth streaming from the throne of God, the lesser things will be of no use. In that fullness of knowledge, the partial know-ledge which we may possess here, true as far as it goes, will then be found useless; just as things which were suitable to us as children are now of little or no use to us in adult life [1 Cor-inthians 13:11]. There is, after all, so little that we can fully and really know here below. What we now see are but the reflec-tions from an imperfect mirror, which clouds and confuses things so that we can only guess at the realities [1 Corinthians 13:12]. We must yield ourselves up to the guidance of Christian love, that we may grow in the true and enduring knowledge.

#### THE CAVE
#### AND THE TRUTH

In Plato's famous allegory of the cave, the men imprisoned there see only the dancing shadows on the wall before them, caused by the puppets of men and animals manipulated by the showman standing behind these men. So fascinated are the men in the cave by the shadowy show before them that it is hard to convince them to turn around and see the showman and the puppets and the firelight that are casting the shadows on the wall. Still more difficult is it to get them to come out of the cave, into the light of day, that they may behold the reality in the world outside. When they do come out into the sunlight, their eyes are so weak that they can only gaze on the ground. Finally their sight grows strong enough so they can look up and see the glory of the heavens and the sun shining there.

We, in this life are like the men imprisoned in the cave. "For our knowledge is imperfect." Science can show us but a little of the truth; theology can tell us very little. It cannot reveal to us the wonder of the vision of God. Yet, even on earth, God allows us to know all we need to know. The one thing we need to know is the wonder and beauty of the law of love, revealed to us in Jesus Christ.

Finally let us think a little about the "things that remain"— the things that are eternal. Faith, hope and love—just these three—will abide forever.

St. Paul tells us quite definitely that even in heaven all three of these greatest virtues—faith, hope, and love—will endure. The well-known hymn by Bishop Christopher Wordsworth, seems to say that faith and hope will disappear in heaven and only love will remain:

> Faith will vanish into sight;
> Hope be emptied in delight;
> Love in heaven will shine more
>      bright;
> Therefore give us love.

However, that is not what St. Paul says in the epistle. Faith and hope and love will all go on. All three will abide. All three will endure.

Faith, to be sure, will be *transformed* in heaven. It will not be by our lower earthly faith that we shall behold the King in his beauty. It will not be by worldly knowledge that we shall know him there. It will be by faith working through love, faith illumined by love, faith looking through the eyes of love. "In thy light do we see light" [Psalm 36:9]. By means of the light which comes from God, as the mystical commentators interpret the words of the psalm, we shall be enabled to see the light which is eternal. We shall be enabled to see God by means of God's own gift to us. God is seen by means of God's own

light, which is the light of love.
The faith that abides in heaven
will be a loving faith.

The hope which remains will
be an eternal hope, and eternal
loving trust which cannot pass
away. Thus eternal faith and
hope find their meaning and
support in the love which transforms them. But love itself
needs no explanation, needs no
support. Love alone, of the
things which abide, is self-
sufficient for love does not behold the divine love as something
outside itself. Love does not
hope for and cling in trust to the
divine as beyond itself. Love *is*
the divine. Love belongs to
God's essence. God *is* love.
That is why the greatest and the
best of these three eternal things
is love.

"If I have prophetic powers,
and understand all mysteries and
all knowledge, and if I have all
faith . . . but have not love, I am
nothing" [1 Corinthians 13:2].
Knowledge of all mysteries, by
itself, cannot bring me any
nearer to God; but if I can learn
to love, even a little, I shall be
able to touch him even now.

We know thee now in part, a portion small,
But love thee as thou art, the all in all;
For reason, and the rays thereof
Are starlight to the noon of love.

## Chapter 7

## THE LIVING BREAD

*Indeed, after this discourse
many of his disciples drew back and no longer
went about with him.*

### The Bread that Gives Life

*John 6:27, 33, 35   Do not
labor for the food which perishes, but for the food which
endures to eternal life, which the
Son of man will give to you; for
on him has God the Father set
his seal. . . . The bread of God is
that which comes down from
heaven, and gives life to the
world. . . . Jesus said to them,
"I am the bread of life; he who
comes to me shall not hunger,
and he who believes in me shall
never thirst!"*

In order to live, it is necessary
to eat. Our physical life must be
sustained by material food, but
"Man shall not live by bread
alone" [Matthew 4:4]. Our

spiritual life requires sustenance
also. So, contrasting these two
kinds of food, our Lord counsels
us here, "Do not labor for the
food which perishes, but for the
food which endures to eternal
life." In the Sermon on the
Mount we read, "Do not lay up
for yourselves treasures on earth,
where moth and rust consume
and where thieves break in and
steal, but lay up for yourselves
treasures in heaven" [Matthew
6:19, 20].

The advice is the same in both
places, though given in different
forms. "Do not spend all your
time, energy, and thought in
working for and amassing the
things that perish." Yet that is
exactly what most people do.

What a vast amount of time and energy is given to the amassing of a fortune, for example. Behind it all is the thought that, in the end, the money gathered together will bring happiness. Instead, how very often it brings only bitterness and disillusionment. Most of us have known instances of the truth of this.

### THE DISCIPLINES
### NECESSARY TO LEARN

In contrast with this, how little time is given by most people to laying up those spiritual treasures which can and do bring enduring joys. Young people devote themselves assiduously to the necessary disciplines involved in learning to play the piano or to draw or paint or even to excel in tennis, golf, or bridge. But how few people, young or old, are willing to devote half an hour or even fifteen minutes a day to learning something of the divine art of prayer? When the time comes to leave the world, mere human arts or skills will not help much, but for the life to come prayer will help a great deal.

In the prayer that our Lord gave us, he taught us to say, "Give us this day our daily bread" [Matthew 6:11]. That means, in the first place, exactly and literally what it says. Bread, material bread, is a necessity for our natural life. So our Lord encourages us to pray for this needed food that we may have the health and strength to meet the duties of each day. We need that daily material bread. We must not forget, however, that we need also "the bread that endureth to eternal life."

Let us not be like that rich farmer in the parable who thought only of the abundant crops in his barns and left God and the things of God out of the picture. God, we remember, called him "Fool!"

"So is he," said our Lord, "who lays up treasure for himself, and is not rich toward God" [Luke 12:16–21].

"The bread of God is that which comes down from heaven, and gives life to the world." Some of the crowds that gathered around Jesus on the other side of the Lake of Galilee, after the miracle of the feeding of the multitude, had apparently not been present at that miraculous occurrence. Now, drawn by curiosity, they wished to see with their own eyes some wonder done by this strange prophet. So they said to him, "What sign do you do, that we may see and believe you? What work do you perform? [John 6:30].

They went on to refer to the manna given for food to their forefathers in the wilderness.

Quoting from the long thanksgiving given in the book of Nehemiah, they refer to this manna as the "bread from heaven" [John 6:31].

But our Lord corrects them. The manna was not truly heavenly bread. It was given by God as a divine gift, just as all good and beautiful and holy things are divine gifts from God. Nevertheless the manna, given in answer to Moses' prayer, was not "the true bread from heaven."

### NEVER TO HUNGER OR THIRST

The true bread from heaven, given by God, does not merely "come down from heaven," but, more wonderfully, it brings heaven itself down to earth. The bread of God is Jesus himself—a Person. He not only comes down from heaven, but also gives true heavenly life to the world. The bread of God came down from heaven to earth on the first Christmas day and lay in a manger. Incarnate God, the Bread of God, came to Bethlehem, "the house of bread." As St. John says [1:14], "The Word became flesh and dwelt among us, full of grace and truth; we have beheld his glory."

So the bread of God, which is Jesus Christ, does not merely sustain natural life in a supernatural way, as the manna did. The bread of God gives life to the world. That is to say, it enables us by partaking of it—or rather of Him—to enter into the true supernatural, undying, heavenly life. For true life is not the life of the world, but eternal life, the life of God himself. St. John sets forth this truth in his first Epistle, "God gave us eternal life, and this life is in his Son. He who has the Son has life; he who has not the Son has not life" [1 John 5:11, 12].

Because of this, our Lord can go on to say, "He who comes to me shall not hunger, and he who believes in me shall never thirst" [John 6:35]. At the beginning of the Sermon on the Mount, he pronounces the blessedness of those "who hunger and thirst after righteousness, for they shall be satisfied" [Matthew 5:6]. Before our desires can be satisfied, we must first experience the desire. If eating and drinking are to bring satisfaction, we must first know hunger and thirst. We need to know spiritual hunger and thirst, hunger and thirst for righteousness and realize that these can be satisfied only by God himself.

The Psalmist cries out, "O God, thou art my God, I seek thee, my soul thirsts for thee; my flesh faints for thee, as in a dry and weary land where no water is" [Psalm 63:1, 2]. He means that earthly joys and earthly happiness can never really satisfy us. The world without God is simply "a dry and weary land where no water is." The human heart will always be restless and unsatisfied until it finally rests in God, its maker. St. Augustine expressed the truth perfectly in the opening words of his *Confessions:* "Thou hast made us for Thyself, O God, and restless are our hearts until they rest in Thee."

So we must come to Jesus, and in him we shall find our needs and longings satisfied. Coming to him, we shall no longer hunger for he is the true bread from heaven. In him too we shall find that our spiritual thirst is quenched, for, as he told the woman of Samaria, "Whoever drinks of the water that I shall give him will never thirst; the water that I shall give him will become in him a spring of water welling up to eternal life" [John 4:14].

The tragedy of much of the world's sin consists in the attempt to find satisfaction for deep basic human longings in things which can give at best only a momentary and partial satisfaction and which end in disappointment, disillusion, or even disgust and remorse. The glutton, the drunkard, the man or woman given over to sensual pleasures, all these are seeking in the passing pleasures of the world that satisfaction—that rest and happiness—which can be found only in God as revealed in Jesus Christ. How truly tragic, how piteous it all is!

"He who comes to me," said Jesus, "shall not hunger, and he who believes in me shall never thirst." In the ancient Breviary Hymn appointed for Lauds on Monday, one of the stanzas reads:

And Christ, our daily food, be
    nigh,
And faith our daily cup supply;
    So may we quaff, to calm and
    bless,
    The Spirit's rapturous holiness.

"Give us this day our daily bread." Give us, dear Lord, day by day, what is needful for our daily life here on earth. Give us also day by day, to revive our spirits and to refresh our souls, the bread of life, that bread of God which comes down from heaven and gives life to the world—the living bread, our Savior, Jesus Christ.

## The Bread
## Which Came Down
## from Heaven

*John 6:51, 57, 58  "I am the living bread which came down from heaven; if any one eats of this bread, he will live for ever; and the bread which I shall give for the life of the world is my flesh. . . . As the living Father sent me, and I live because of the Father, so he that eats me will live because of me. This is the bread which came down from heaven, not such as the fathers ate and died; he who eats this bread will live forever."*

"I am the living bread." The discourse in the synagogue at Capernaum could not be fully understood by those who heard it until finally, at the Last Supper, "Jesus took bread, and blessed, and broke it, and gave it to the disciples and said, 'Take, eat; this is my body' " [Matthew 26:26]. No wonder that many of those at Capernaum "disputed among themselves, saying, 'How can this man give us his flesh to eat?' " Indeed, "many of his disciples" who had been following him, after this discourse, "drew back and no longer went about with him" [John 6:52, 66]. It required "blind" faith at that time to accept the teachings of Jesus.

HOW CAN THIS BE?

We can eat of the living bread which came down from heaven and which is likewise "the flesh of the Son of man" [John 6:53] only because of the real, sacramental presence of our Lord in the Holy Eucharist. "How can this man give us his flesh to eat?"

The answer is that he could not possibly do so if he were merely man. Only because he is also God is it possible for him to feed us with his flesh—his body—as the food for our souls and the means of building up our spiritual life. This is a divine mystery, as St. Thomas Aquinas says,

Word-made-flesh, true bread he
    maketh
 By his word his Flesh to be,
Wine his Blood; which whoso
    taketh
    Must from carnal thoughts be
    free;
Faith alone, though sight for-
    saketh,
 Shows true hearts the mystery.
        [St. Thomas Aquinas
            Hymn 199]

The mystery is accomplished only because he is indeed the living bread from heaven, the Word made flesh. So as in faith we approach the altar and receive into our bodies the outward and visible signs of bread and wine, we also receive in and through them the inward and spiritual grace, the real but glorified Body and Blood of our Lord. So he himself can become our own true inward self, and his own divine life can give divine power to our lives here on earth. Every time we receive Holy Communion, we ought to make our own the words of St. Paul, "It is no longer

I who live, but Christ who lives in me" [Galatians 2:20].

"Lord, evermore give us this bread" [John 6:34].

The mere outward reception of the Blessed Sacrament is, of course, not enough. It must be accompanied always by a lively faith in our Lord, "discerning the body," as St. Paul says [1 Corinthians 11:29]. Also we must have a real desire that Christ will take hold of us by means of Holy Communion and transform our sinful bodies into the sinless likeness to himself and change our sinful lives into the likeness of his holy life, "that we may evermore dwell in him, and he in us" [Prayer of Humble Access, *Book of Common Prayer,* p. 82].

"As the living Father sent me, and I live because of the Father, so he that eats me will live because of me." We are, then, not only to receive our Lord in the Holy Sacrament, but we are to live in and by him. We are to live the eucharistic life. We are to feed on him, not only at the moment of the reception of Holy Communion, but we are to continue to feed on him constantly. We need to be feeding always on the Bread of Life in order to preserve our true, our spiritual, our supernatural life.

The sacramental feeding on Christ is, of course, necessary for us. By devout reception of Holy Communion, the Incarnate Word is, as it were, reincarnated in each one of us. He becomes the sustenance of our souls, his own life enters into us. To this sacramental feeding especially his words apply, "Unless you eat the flesh of the Son of man and drink his blood, you have no life in you" [John 6:53]. We must not forget that in addition to this sacramental feeding, it is also possible to feed on Christ in other ways.

IN THY HEART
BY FAITH
WITH THANKSGIVING

There is the mystical feeding on our Lord Jesus through prayer and contemplation. The second half of the long formula of administration for the Consecrated Bread, printed in Anglican Prayer Books for so many years, read, "Take and eat this in remembrance that Christ died for thee, and feed on him in thy heart by faith, with thanksgiving" [*Book of Common Prayer,* p. 82]. These words, emphasizing the more subjective side of the act of Communion, nevertheless state an important truth. It is indeed necessary that we feed on Jesus Christ in our hearts if we are to know the full power and strength that he intends us to receive in Holy Communion. St. Luke, speaking of the birth of our Lord in Bethlehem, tells us that "Mary kept all these things, pondering them in her heart" [Luke 2:19]. Many people went through the experience of seeing the child, Jesus. The blessed Mother, though, kept and pondered these things in her heart, so they became fully effective in her. Thus we must practice this inward mystical feeding on Christ as well as outwardly partaking of the Bread and Wine in the Holy Eucharist.

We need also to meditate daily on the Word of God as that Word is presented to us in the Holy Scriptures. "It is they that bear witness to me," says our Lord [John 5:39]. If we read the Scriptures with devotion and meditate upon them faithfully, they will lead us to him. So then, in the Bible we can find the adorable presence of Christ and in our reading and meditation we find another way of feeding on him in our hearts, by faith, with thanksgiving.

A third way in which we can feed on Christ is by what might be called the moral, or ethical, way. In the Blessed Sacrament, the very power of Christ himself is imparted to us. Divine grace, divine strength is given to us. We must then be careful to exercise that power. We must ourselves "do the works of Christ." We must try to practice acts of love

to all mankind. This is truly to feed on him. The bread of God, strengthening us, enables us to work for God's glory and for our neighbor's benefit. All our natural actions are transformed by the love of Christ working within us. Humdrum, difficult, tiresome things are transfigured. "Drudgery becomes divine" as George Herbert put it [Hymn 476].

A final blessing of our feeding on the Living Bread is set before us in the words, "He who eats this bread will live for ever" [John 6:58]. Christ imparts to us the gift of eternal life. To live forever, in the sense of having our present life prolonged indefinitely, is a prospect which may seem far from attractive if it is to be interpreted as an endless lengthening of earthly existence, with its burdens of cares and darknesses and doubts. To "live for ever" suggests too readily the tedium and monotony that we too often experience in the succession of weary days, one after another.

But the eternal life which comes to us in Christ is life of a different quality, a different kind of life, lifted up above and freed from the weariness of mere succession of days. This eternal life, to be gained in its fullness in heaven, can still, in a measure, be ours here and now. Here we cannot experience it continuously;

but we may still glimpse something of its wonder from time to time. Experience of eternal life is that quiet but intense joy which may come to us momentarily at certain times in our lives. It is akin to that sense of rapture which we find in reunion with a dear friend after long years of separation. Or we may compare it to the sudden lifting of our spirits which we may find in a wonderful view from a mountaintop or in beholding a great work of art or in listening to sublime music or in the inward peace and joy which sometimes comes to us in receiving Holy Communion or experiencing the presence of God in times of prayer. All these suggest to us something of the quality of eternal life, though eternal life itself is greater far than these. Eternal life is the constant and ceaseless experience of the joy and peace and rapture of which we have been speaking.

"If any one eats of this bread, he will live for ever." For eternal life, finally, is the life of Jesus Christ himself, the life which he now experiences in his glorified humanity at the right hand of the Father. We are to share in and know this eternal heavenly life as united to him. "In thy presence," says the Psalmist, "there is fullness of joy, in thy right hand are pleasures for evermore" [Psalm 16:11]. These are the priceless treasures of eternal life and eternal love which are in Christ and which come to us through Christ. As we feed on him, day by day, we become transformed into his likeness. Well may we pray with those disciples, "Lord, give us this bread always."

## Chapter 8

## RESURRECTION APPEARANCES

*St. Thomas is often referred to as*
*"the doubting Thomas."*
*This seems to me to be a mistaken judgment of him.*

### St. Thomas

*John 20:24-29  Now Thomas, one of the twelve, called the Twin, was not with them when Jesus came. So the other disciples told him, "We have seen the Lord." But he said to them, "Unless I see in his hands the print of the nails, and place my finger in the mark of the nails, and place my hand in his side, I will not believe."*

*Eight days later, his disciples were again in the house, and Thomas was with them. The doors were shut, but Jesus came and stood among them, and said, "Peace be with you." Then he said to Thomas, "Put your finger here, and see my hands; and put*

*out your hand, and place it in my side; do not be faithless but believing." Thomas answered him, "My Lord and my God!" Jesus said to him, "Have you believed because you have seen me? Blessed are those who have not seen and yet believe."*

Thomas was not with them when Jesus came at first. We are not told why. Nevertheless, the fact that he was not with the others was his loss. St. Thomas was a devoted follower of our Lord, but a bit inclined to pessimism, always ready to expect the worst and tending to look on the dark side. When our Lord suggested that he go to Bethany to visit the tomb of Lazarus, Thomas immediately responded, "Let us also go, that we may die with him" [John 11:16]. He thought that death for all of them was inevitable, yet bravely wished to accompany Jesus. So, on this day after the resurrection, when Jesus appeared to the others, it was a mistake for Thomas to be off by himself with the companionship of his gloomy thoughts.

From Thomas's absence, we may learn the lesson of the importance of our shared community life as Christians. When Adam was alone in the garden, God said, "It is not good that the man should be alone; I will make him a helper for him" [Genesis 2:18]. It is still true that it is not good for man, or woman either, to be alone. It is very likely to lead to discouragement, morbidity, or disagreeable selfishness. We are reminded of the fact that the great St. Benedict of Nursia began his Religious life as a hermit, by himself in a cave. Later he abandoned solitude and, instead, established life in a community, finding that the solitary life gave no real opportunity to learn patience and charity. To learn to live lovingly and happily with others is a basic need for Christians.

It is within and through a group of believers that Jesus manifests his resurrection presence and power. Only when Thomas rejoins his community is he granted the vision of the risen Lord. Do we, perhaps, try to live in selfish isolation from our fellow members in Christ? Do we neglect to go out in love and sympathy to our brethren? If so, we are missing those treasures of spiritual power which can come to us only in fellowship, only in the *communion* of saints.

St. Thomas is often referred to as "the doubting Thomas," the very symbol of unbelief and lack of faith. This seems to me to be a mistaken judgment of him. On the contrary, Thomas was a man of real faith and trust in our Lord, and of love for Jesus Christ. It was just because of this great love and the eagerness of his faith that he hesitated to accept the fact of the resurrection without, as it seemed to him, adequate proof. The other apostles, it is true, had said, "We have seen the Lord," but their testimony did not bring to him the personal assurance that he longed for and did not satisfy his own desire to share in a real way in their own experience.

Our Lord himself had warned his disciples against too great credulity. "If any one says to you, 'Look, here is the Christ!' or 'Look, there he is!' do not believe it" [Mark 13:21].

Credulity is not the same as faith. Readiness to accept claims of strange or unaccountable happenings as proof of religion does not indicate a true religious spirit.

St. Thomas was right in expecting experience to make faith firm and possible for him. What was wrong was for him to lay down the particular means of proof he wished. He demanded a materialistic, naturalistic proof, capable of convincing the senses. "Unless I see . . . the print of the nails, and place my finger in the mark of the nails, . . . I will not believe" [John 20:25]. The combined evidence of the senses (sight and touch), so Thomas thought, would be necessary to bring conviction that Jesus had truly risen.

The fact remains that sight and touch alone could never prove to Thomas, or anyone else, the reality of the living Christ, the resurrected Jesus, the living Lord. Sight and touch might serve to identify a dead body, but never the living and glorified Jesus. Our senses cannot attain to the greatest things in life—the reality beyond all appearances. "The things that are seen are transient, but the things that are unseen are eternal" [2 Corinthians 4:18].

So, as it turned out, the basis of Thomas's faith was supplied by something quite different from the "proof" that he had demanded. What brought him

faith was the fact that the risen Jesus could read the secret thoughts of the heart of Thomas. "Then Jesus said to Thomas, 'Put your finger here, and see my hands; and put out your hand, and place it in my side; do not be faithless, but believing' " [John 20:27]. Our Lord was not visibly there when Thomas laid down his conditions. But Jesus now bids him do exactly what he had said he wanted to do. It was the voice of Jesus, the familiar speech, and the searching of Thomas's heart, the knowledge of all its secrets, that brought conviction to him.

The proof of our religion lies in the assurance that God in Christ can and does speak to our inmost souls. "Have you believed because you have seen me?" asked our Lord of Thomas. He went on, "Blessed are those who have not seen and yet believe" [John 20:29]. Was the sense of sight the source of Thomas's faith? Was it the placing of his finger in the mark of the nails, the thrusting of his hand into the wounded side that brought conviction to him, that caused him to cry out, "My Lord and my God"? I think that we may be very sure that Thomas did not touch the risen Lord at all. He understood that that would not do. It would be impious, a desecration. No, Thomas did not put his finger into the pierced hands, nor did he put his hand into the wounded side, as he had declared he must and would do, before he could believe. Nor did faith come to him simply because the other disciples declared that they had seen Jesus. He came to believe because of the personal, spiritual, secret action of the voice and presence of Jesus in his own soul.

So, too, faith comes to us not by visions of Christ made manifest to our outward senses. It comes instead by prayer, by contemplation, by the touch of Christ on our souls in the sacraments of the Church, by the coming of Jesus in the Holy Communion. "He who believes in the Son of God has the testimony in himself" [1 John 5:10]. We believe not merely on the basis of the apostolic testimony given to us in the Scriptures, nor because of the even greater witness of the Church. We believe because of the personal touch of Jesus on our souls, because of the personal experience of his love. We come to learn the truth as it is in Christ Jesus through the convincing power of the experience of our soul's rest in Jesus. We are to "taste and see, how gracious the Lord is" [Psalm 34:8].

Faith is not the mere intellectual acceptance of a number of creedal statements. In this sense,

we are reminded, "Even the demons believe—and shudder" [James 2:19]. They know the truths of the Christian religion— and wish that they were not true. True faith means, "I know *whom* I have believed" [2 Timothy 1:12], that I have loved him and touched him, not by putting a finger into the mark of the nails, but through the supernatural energies of prayer. True faith means that I have had the experience of the living Christ in my soul, and, because of that experience—so true and deep and real—I will cling to Christ always, no matter what may happen to me. "Who shall separate us from the love of Christ?" [Romans 8:35].

"I will see you again and your hearts will rejoice, and no one will take your joy from you" [John 16:22]. No one can take our Christian joy away from us because our joy is based on faith and hope in the living God and the personal experience of the power of the living Jesus. That is something which is ours and belongs to us. No man has given it to us, and no man can take it from us.

## The Varied Appearances

*John 20:30-31  Now Jesus did many other signs in the presence of the disciples, which are not written in this book; but these are written that you may believe*

*that Jesus is the Christ, the Son
of God, and that believing you
may have life in his name.*

"Jesus did many other signs."
In that connection let us think of
the meaning of all the varied sort
of appearances that our Lord
made to his disciples after the
resurrection. These appearances,
so different from one another
in their circumstances and other
aspects, were intended to meet
the varied spiritual needs of
those to whom he showed himself. So to Mary Magdalene he
appeared as a gardener [John
20:11-18]. To the two disciples
on their way to Emmaus, he
appeared as a fellow pilgrim,
walking with them along the
road, an ever-present companion
[Luke 24:13-27]. To the disciples assembled behind locked
doors in the upper room "for
fear of the Jews" he brings a
message of peace and security
[John 20:19-23]. To
St. Thomas, as we have seen, he
manifests himself as searcher of
thoughts and of the heart and
finally as incarnate God himself,
as Thomas makes his great confession, "My Lord and my God"
[John 20:26-29].

PARTIAL AND INCOMPLETE

Let us try to learn from these
varied appearances of the risen
Lord to his disciples that our
own individual conceptions of

the glory and power and
presence of Jesus are always but
partial and incomplete. Our own
conceptions of what our Lord
Jesus Christ is must ever remain
inadequate to grasp his inconceivable majesty. No matter how
far we may have advanced in our
spiritual life, there still remains
much to be learned of the
unsearchable riches of Christ. No
matter how far we may have pro-
gressed in growing in the love of
Christ, there is still much to learn
of that "love of Christ which
surpasses knowledge" [Ephesians
3:19]. So we must pray that
our vision may be enlarged and
that we may come to see and
know him in ways that are as yet
unguessed at because of our
present blindness and ignorance.

Let us ask our Lord for whole-
ness of vision, for true catholic-
ity of faith, that we may grow
day by day in the knowledge and
love of God and of his blessed
Son by study, by prayer, by contemplation, and, most important-
ly, by living the life of love. Let
us hope and believe that our
Lord will make himself known to
us in new and unexpected ways.
In this connection, Father
Benson has written:

We must not look to see
Jesus in the ways of natural
expectation. His presence is
not of this world. The worldly
heart cannot anticipate the

modes in which he will work. We dwarf the channels of his approach by endeavoring to mark out beforehand in what ways he will come.

We must not think that human wisdom will enable us to see him. We cannot lay down the conditions of his manifestation.

It is the eye of love which perceives the presence of Jesus. We must be constantly watching for him, content even though we do not seem to find him, patient amidst the discipline which he appoints.

The eye of love will never be forgetful of the object for which it waits. In everything it perceives his presence, and the manifold veils of earthly form beneath which it is conscious of his approach serve but to show forth the varied fullness of his being. They are diverse one from another, but in all of them he is glorified. Their multiplicity suits our imperfection while it makes known the perfection which is in him.

We must not be satisfied with any one of the ways whereby Jesus is to be found. We must seek him in all the ways by which he approaches us. He who comes is complete in all: but we who receive fail to receive him truly in those ways in which we seek him, because

we seek him not also in those other ways which are essential to our obtaining a real grasp of his spiritual glory.

At all times and in all places we must be seeking him. We fail to see him if we think there is any place where he cannot be seen. He is seen not because circumstances are favorable, but because he shows himself. He shows himself wherever he wills to those who look to him with love [*Life Beyond the Grave,* pp. 481–482].

We still, then, have much to learn of Jesus. Only in the Beatific Vision, when, like him, we shall see him as he is [1 John 3:2] shall we see him fully.

### THE UNHAPPY DIVISIONS AMONG CHRISTIANS

How often the littleness of men's minds and understanding have tried to separate these varying revelations of Jesus' presence and love and make them into a series of contradictory appearances, so as to declare that, if we recognize him in one particular way, then it must follow that it is impossible for others to experience his presence in a different way! That is one of the causes of the unhappy divisions among Christians. It is as though those travelers to Emmaus, who experienced the companionship of Jesus as a fellow pilgrim, should declare that it was impossible that Mary Magdalene should have beheld him the in guise of the gardener. Or that, because the risen Lord showed himself to the assembly of the apostles, it was therefore impossible for him to manifest himself to individuals.

So some who find Jesus in the Scriptures think it impossible for others to find him in the Eucharist. Still others who experience his presence in the individual heart do not see how others can find him in the Church. Others, stressing his true humanity, find it impossible to accept his equally true deity. How much better it would be if we could learn to accept *all* the revelations of God's presence and *all* the wonders of Jesus' love! How much better for all of us if we would become more truly catholic—in the real sense of that word.

"But there are also many other things which Jesus did; were every one of them to be written, I suppose that the world itself could not contain the books that would be written" [John 21:25]. Things which, therefore, you and I know nothing about, but he did them just the same! Let us praise God for the many manifestations we ourselves have known of Jesus' presence and power and love. Let us praise him also for the countless other manifestations of the same presence and power and love made to others of our fellow Christians ("our separated brethren," if you like). Further let us praise him for revealing himself in some measure to many who do not "profess and call themselves Christians" at all.

Let us praise God that Christ reveals himself to us in the sacrament of nature's beauty, manifesting himself to us through his creatures. Let us recognize his presence in the mystery of prayer. Let us learn to find Jesus in the pages of the Gospel, and let the Holy Scriptures bring to us the ever-present Christ. Let us seek to know him better as he stands in the midst of his Church, mediating his power to us through the sacraments which his love has ordained. Let us seek and find him also in the hearts and lives of our fellow Christians —yes, in the hearts and lives of all our fellow men—especially in the poor and weak and suffering, in the unloving and unlovely. If we cannot find Jesus in the hearts of our fellows, there is something terribly wrong.

Let us try to find Jesus in all the events of our life. Let us try to find him in the painful and dreaded events, as well as in all the pleasant and treasured events. Indeed we ought to find him more especially in the painful events, for the road to Calvary, the way of the Cross, was a pain-

ful way in which Jesus himself
walked.

### The Restoration of the Penitent

*John 21:15-22 When they had
finished breakfast, Jesus said to
Simon Peter, "Simon, son of
John, do you love me more than
these?" He said to him, "Yes,
Lord; you know that I love
you." He said to him, "Feed my
lambs." A second time he said
to him, "Simon, son of John, do
you love me?" He said to him,
"Yes, Lord; you know that I love
you." He said to him, "Tend my
sheep." He said to him the third
time, "Simon, son of John, do
you love me?" Peter was grieved
because he said to him the third
time, "Do you love me?" And
he said to him, "Lord, you know
everything; you know that I love
you." Jesus said to him, "Feed
my sheep. Truly, truly, I say to
you, when you were young, you
girded yourself and walked
where you would; but when you
are old, you will stretch out your
hands, and another will gird you
and carry you where you do not
wish to go." (This he said to
show by what death he was to
glorify God.) And after this he
said to him, "Follow me."*

*Peter turned and saw following
them the disciple whom Jesus
loved, who had lain close to his
breast at the supper and had said,
"Lord, who is it that is going to
betray you?" When Peter saw
him, he said to Jesus, "Lord,
what about this man?" Jesus
said to him, "If it is my will that
he remain until I come, what is
that to you? Follow me!"*

TO BE SORRY FOR OUR SINS
IS NOT ENOUGH

Three times Peter had denied
his Lord, saying, "I do not know
the man." So now the risen
Savior, for each offense of Peter,
demands an acknowledgment of
love on the part of the erring
apostle. But more than this!
Acknowledgment of love in
words must be demonstrated
in deeds. Acts of reparation
must follow the words of devotion. To be sorry for our sins
and failures is not enough. We
must resolve, with God's help to
do better, and we must show in
our lives the signs of true repen-
tance.

So the dialogue goes on in this
way.

"Do you love me?"

"Yes, Lord, you know that I
love you."

"Very well, then, feed my
lambs . . . tend my sheep . . . feed
my sheep. Demonstrate by your
love and care for your brethren,
both small and great, your love
for me."

The way to show our love to
Jesus is to show our love and

care for our brothers and sisters in Christ.

It is true, of course, that in one sense the evil consequences of our sins and betrayals cannot be undone. Yet our Lord's pardoning love and grace do make it possible for us to gain a victory over our failures in love by earnestly trying to go out in acts of love towards our brethren. "As you did it to one of the least of my brethren, you did it to me" [Matthew 25:40]. The love of the penitent heart for Jesus Christ must be expressed in constant acts of love and thoughtfulness towards other members of the flock of the great Shepherd. For every act of failure, Jesus calls us to perform an act of love. St. Peter's threefold denial calls out the threefold command to feed and tend the flock.

St. Paul, thinking of the consequences of Adam's sin, assures us that "where sin increased, grace abounded all the more" [Romans 5:20]. Man's sin could never drown out God's love— God's grace. The love of God is always greater than the sin of man. What is true of the whole human race can be true in our individual lives. Our sins are many and great, but God's grace as manifested in the love we show to others should abound all the more. The Christian vocation demands that we care

for and love and help others. "Bear one another's burdens, and so fulfill the law of Christ" [Galatians 6:2].

So, having pardoned his transgression, Jesus says to Peter, "Follow me!" The words are the very same that the Lord spoke at the beginning, when he first called Peter to be his disciple. Human voices change, but the voice of the eternal Word is ever the same. Every day that voice of the eternal Word says to each one of us, "Follow me!"

The same voice and the same words spoken to Peter by the lakeside, when Jesus first called him, are now heard again by Peter, but, in view of all that has happened since the first time he heard the words, how much more full of meaning to Peter is the summons to follow Jesus! Peter understands better now than when he started out all that is involved in following Jesus. So we too ought to be growing day by day, through our experience of the love of Jesus, in the knowledge of what it means to follow him.

### AND THE OTHERS? WHAT ABOUT THEM?

Then Peter, always impulsive, notices that John, the beloved disciple, is also following Jesus.

"Lord, what about this man? What is to happen to him?" We

need not suppose that mere idle curiosity prompted the question. It was a natural question, based on the kindly human desire to have his friend and fellow disciple included in the invitation and call that he had just received. Surely it must be the will of Jesus to include the beloved disciple in faithful following right up to the end, even to a martyrdom like Peter's, by which he too would "glorify God"! But John's vocation was to be different from Peter's.

So it is with us. It is natural for us to assume that, because our Lord calls us along a certain path—perhaps to an active life of service or perhaps to a more hidden life of prayer or of suffering—it is natural for us to think that, in order to follow Jesus, others too must necessarily follow in the same path. Yes, this is natural, but it is probably mistaken. So our Lord gently rebukes Peter.

"If I will that he remain until I come [if I will that he have a different vocation from yours], what is that to you?" His vocation, like yours, is in accordance with my will. His vocation does not change your own vocation, your own duties, that have been shown to you. "Follow thou me!"

My own vocation, my own following of Christ, is not to be judged or decided by the vocations of others. I must follow faithfully in the path that Christ has marked out for me. Others may be called to walk in other paths, but I must persevere in the place and in the work that God has made known to me. What others do, or do not do, cannot alter my vocation or excuse my unfaithfulness to my vocation.

"What is that to you? Follow me!"

We must not then be envious or jealous of the work or place or different vocation that God may have given to others. Peter and John were both apostles. The vocation of Peter was to follow Jesus to death on the cross. John's vocation, on the other hand, was to wait in loving contemplation until Jesus should come to take him to himself at the end of a long, long life.

There was one thing in common in the differing vocations of Peter and John. Both were called upon to suffer. Perhaps, in many ways, the long waiting and the weariness to which St. John was called were more difficult to bear than the sharp pains of crucifixion endured by St. Peter. But both paths—both vocations—led to the same heaven. We must walk in that particular path that our Lord has assigned to us. If he wants us to wait in patience, we must wait. If he wants us, like Peter, to lay down our lives for him, then we must accept death in trustful love.

I HAVE MADE, AND
I WILL BEAR

In another appearance of Jesus, made to the eleven apostles in Galilee, our Lord assured them, "Lo, I am with you always, to the close of the age" [Matthew 28:20]. The realization of the presence of our Lord with us in every circumstance of life will be to us a source of great strength. It will carry us on through every difficulty. As we grow old and experience the increasing infirmities that come with the years, we shall find that Christ's final words to Peter apply to each one of us also.

"When you were young, you girded yourself and walked where you would; but when you are old, . . . another will gird you and carry you where you do not wish to go" [John 21:18]. We shall not be "girded" or bound to be carried to a literal cross, as was St. Peter; but, nevertheless, we shall truly be bound—girded—by increasing weakness, pains of sickness, perhaps loss of hearing or sight. These "bindings" are for us a cross, and by them, like St. Peter, we can glorify God.

If we can only remember this, it makes it so much easier!

Through all these increasing disabilities; through every difficulty that we may find at any time of our life in our efforts to carry out God's will for us—through all these things we are glorifying God, and he is sanctifying us.

After all, the prophet Isaiah assures us that the one who is "carrying us," even though it seem to be to a place "where we do not wish to go," is none other than *God himself*. "Even to your old age, I am he, and to gray hairs will I carry you. I have made, and I will bear; I will carry and will save" [Isaiah 46:4]. That is the promise. God himself will carry us. In his arms we are safe. Let us make our own those familiar words of the great St. Theresa,

Let nothing disturb thee,
Let nothing affright thee,
All things are passing
God never changeth;
Patient endurance attaineth to
    all things;
Whom God possesseth nothing
    is wanting,
Alone God sufficeth.

As he said at the beginning, "Follow me," so he still says now, "Follow me." So he will say at the end when he opens to us the gates of Paradise and brings us to the vision of the heavenly glory!

Chapter 9

## VOCATION

## THE CALL OF CHRIST TO THE SOUL

*Why not return to the peaceful village*
*to settle down to do good, to teach, to heal?*

### Looking unto Jesus

*John 17:3 This is eternal life,*
*that they know thee the only*
*true God, and Jesus Christ whom*
*thou hast sent.*

This life-giving knowledge of
God, which brings to us courage
and joy, is not a mere intellectual
kind of knowledge to be acquired
as a result of study. Nor can we
attain to it by our own efforts.
This knowledge is revealed by
God to us "in the face of Jesus
Christ." To be learned in philos-
ophy, to be expert in science,
even to be able to discuss theology profoundly—these things
cannot bring to us eternal life.
Nor can they bring comfort in
pain or encouragement in des-

pondency or rouse us to new
effort when we are slack. The
only source for us of true eternal
life is to behold "the light of the
knowledge of the glory of God in
the face of Christ" [2 Corinthians 4:6]. To have this saving
knowledge of God, the beauty,
the holiness, the courage, and the
boundless love of Jesus must
have touched the soul. Here we
see the unveiling of eternal God
himself.

As those Greeks came to Philip
and said to him, "Sir, we wish to
see Jesus" [John 12:20-21], so,
above all things, let us desire to
see Jesus, whose love alone can
renew and strengthen us. "Shine
once again, O God, in our hearts
to give the light of the know-

82

ledge of thy glory in the face of Christ."

Let us begin by contemplating the eternal creative Word of Life in the bosom of the Father. "In the beginning was the Word, and the Word was with God, and the Word was God" [John 1:1]. That Word was alive, active, energizing in obedience to the Father's will. "All things were made through him, and without him was not anything made. That which has been made was life in him" [John 1:3–4]. All life flows from him by the power of the Holy Spirit, the giver of life. The Word of God is the source of all our being, of all our life. He is the source of our physical life, for through him all things are made. He is also the source of our spiritual and supernatural life, for the Word, by his incarnation, became our redeemer, restoring to us when we had fallen away from God, the possibility of eternal life.

### THE CONTINUING PROCESS OF CREATION

He called the world into existence at the beginning, but the creative Word still calls forth the universe through a continuing process of creation which never stops. The creation story as given in Genesis, taken literally, would seem to indicate that God, having set the world going, ceased from creative activity:

"on the seventh day God finished his work which he had done, and he rested on the seventh day from all his work which he had done" [Genesis 2:2]. But our Lord, when he was reproached for healing the paralyzed man on the Sabbath, corrects this mistaken view. "Jesus answered them, 'My father is working still, and I am working.' " [John 5:17]. Creation still goes on.

My life, then, is of God. It proceeds from the eternal Word, God's Son. At every level it proceeds from eternal life. Physical life, spiritual life, all the gifts of life come from the bounty of the eternal Word of life. He created me, he sustains me; at every moment of my life, he gives me the gifts I need. All this bounty assures me of his eternal love. Surely I am bound to love him in return.

This eternal Word of God, "for us men and for our salvation," became incarnate, was made flesh. "The Word became flesh and dwelt among us, full of grace and truth" [John 1:14]. Divine glory clothes itself in a human body and shows us eternal life in the terms of human life. So it is that we can indeed behold the light of the knowledge of God in the face of Jesus Christ.

To attempt to contemplate the being of God the Holy Trinity is far beyond our powers. "Such knowledge is too wonderful for me; it is high, I cannot attain it" [Psalm 139:6]. But God has condescended to our weakness, and in the Word Incarnate has manifested his Being in human and understandable terms. We look with love on the Babe of Bethlehem. We see the glory of God in the face of the little child Jesus, in the boy in the carpenter's shop, in the prophet of Galilee, and in the scarred and bleeding face of the sufferer on the cross. In all these instances, we behold the glory of God in the face of Jesus Christ.

GOD'S UNDERSTANDING

As we see Jesus facing difficulties and problems similar to those which we ourselves have to meet, we are assured of God's own understanding and sympathy with us in our difficulties. The perfection of the human life of Jesus gives us hope for the perfection of our lives. His humanity is not destroyed or overwhelmed by his divine nature; his life shows us what ours might be if we allowed God's grace and glory to fill our lives as it filled the life of Jesus. For the Father wills through Jesus to bring many sons and daughters to glory. With the help of God's grace, in our place and time, we can ourselves live the holy life that Jesus lived.

Let us think finally of the goodness and compassion of Jesus. Even now he is calling us to come to him. Just as when he was on earth, so now he is ready to receive all who need him—the sinners, the sick, the despairing. He is our Savior. "Come to me, all who labor and are heavy-laden and I will give you rest" [Matthew 11:28]. So he will not refuse us if we try to return to him—return to him with renewed devotion. Hear him saying to us, as he said to his earlier disciples, "Will you also go away? [John 6:67]. In these days of stress and testing, in this time of fiery trial, will you also go away? Will you be unfaithful? Will you be offended?

May there come from us today, as there came from Simon Peter then, the answer, "Lord, to whom shall we go? You have the words of eternal life" [John 6:68]. Yet we do forget so very easily all that Jesus has done for us. We overlook those precious Christian influences which help us so much even when we are unaware of them. We forget the constraining love of Christ.

Consider what the world would be like if (impossibly) Christ had never lived. There would be no Gospels, no New Testament, no Church, no sacraments, no Christian Sundays, no Christian hymns. There would be but an imperfect knowledge of God, and it is doubtful whether we could think of God as love at all. There would be even less unselfishness, more sensuality, more cruelty, even more dependence on force than there is now, less pity for the oppressed, the destitute, for the aged, and for children. These things will be neglected and forgotten by those who forget Jesus Christ. The presence of Christ in the world has brought about most of the good things in the world; just as the presence of Jesus Christ in my way of life has brought about what little of deserving there is in my life.

Let us go forward. Let us open our eyes. Let us return to Jesus to refresh our spirit, to regain the vision. "Come unto me. . . . Take my yoke upon you, and learn from me; . . . and you will find rest for your souls. For my yoke is easy, and my burden is light" [Matthew 11:28-30]. Come unto me. Throw off the heavy yoke of sin, self, and worldliness, and take once again that sweet and blessed and easy yoke of Jesus Christ. Surely the light of the knowledge of the glory of God in the face of Jesus Christ is sufficient for our every need.

## The Call of Jesus

"Lord to whom shall we go? You have the words of eternal life." In him alone is the hope of the world and our own hope. The vision of the attractiveness and loveliness of Jesus Christ is followed by his call to us, "Come unto me." It is not enough that we have once responded to that call, for it is a repeated and continuous call and demands of us a repeated and continuous response. Just as an artist goes again and again to study a great painting or as the scholar goes repeatedly to the library to learn more of his subject, so we should be drawn repeatedly to seek and to study Jesus Christ anew. While there are as many different aspects of the call of Christ as there are different individual men and women, there are certain aspects of Christ's call which are universal.

The call of Jesus is always a call to follow him. So to the Galilean fishermen, Jesus said, " 'Follow me and I will make you become fishers of men.' And immediately they left their nets and followed him" [Mark 1:17-18]. They followed him *immediately* on hearing the call. There is an imperious quality in the call of Jesus. It has a note of immediacy, of priority about it. It must come first and have precedence above business, even above family ties. St. Matthew tells us that when James and John were called, "Immediately they left the [fishing] boat and their father, and followed him" [Matthew 4:22].

Besides its immediacy, the call of Jesus has a certain quality of the unknown about it. "Follow me and I will make you become fishers of men." He does not tell them *where* he will lead them, nor does he explain the strange expression "fishers of men." What could that mean? They knew about fishing for fish, but how could they know that they were equipped for this new kind of fishing? But these unknown factors did not deter them or affect the promptness of their response. The very voice of Jesus who called them brought the assurance that he would empower and equip them for the work he asked them to do. And their trust in him was not disappointed.

### THE SAME BUT DIFFERENT

In following Jesus there is much that we do not know, which we are not supposed to know. It is enough that, if we follow, we shall learn. While the call to follow Christ involves going out to unknown places and undertaking unknown tasks, what he demands of us is of a piece with what we have done before. The fishers of fish were still fishers, although now fishers of men. Natural gifts and talents were transformed and developed but not abolished. Christ takes us as we are and perfects and

transforms us, but he does not make us into different persons. So, when Saul the persecutor becomes Paul the saint, the same zeal remains; but the zeal for persecution has been changed into loving zeal for Christ. Christ, as it were, brings out the grain in our souls, making the wood more beautiful, setting free all our talents for fuller use. The call to follow Jesus is the call to the more abundant life.

### THE ROYAL CROSS

Then the call of Christ is also a call to cross-bearing. "If any man would come after me, let him deny himself and take up his cross and follow me" [Matthew 16:24]. Christ will not deceive us. He makes clear that it is difficult to follow him. There is much happiness in following Jesus, but we cannot avoid the cross. There will be many trials, necessary self-discipline, frequent disappointments and discouragements, little crosses to be borne each day. Perhaps we shall find, as he himself found, a great cross at the end. So, for the Christian, there are days of joy and days of sorrow. Indeed, this is true of all human life. But for the Christian, Christ sanctifies the cross and makes it fruitful. He changes it from a symbol of death into an instrument of life. Christ asks of us nothing that he has not borne himself. Our difficulties and sorrows are, after all, but very little compared to the awfulness of his cross and passion. The way of the cross is also the way of glory. It has truly been called the "Royal Way of the Holy Cross."

PERFECTION

Finally, the call of Jesus to us is the call to perfection. "You, therefore, must be perfect, as your heavenly Father is perfect" [Matthew 5:48]. These words of our Lord in the Sermon on the Mount reecho the command of God given in the ancient Hebrew scriptures, "You shall be holy; for I the Lord your God am holy" [Leviticus 19:2]. Only, now that Christ has come and the Word has been made flesh and the Holy Spirit has been poured out upon us, this perfection has been made possible for us, which before was only an unattainable ideal.

These words of Jesus constitute a commandment for *all* his followers without exception. Very often the "Religious Life" alone is referred to as *the* way of perfection. But it is not the exclusive way of perfection, for the path of life of every single Christian should be a way of perfection. In itself, the Religious Life is not more perfect than other forms of Christian life. The way in which a Christian is to walk depends on Christ's special call to that particular soul. The call to follow Christ, whatever the way, is the call to perfection.

The perfection to which we are called means that we are to be perfect in our sphere of life, even as God is perfect in his infinite and heavenly sphere of life. The call to perfection, then, is not unattainable by us, for Christ is not calling us to be like God, but to be perfect in our human sphere of life as God is perfect in his. We are called to be perfect men, not perfect Gods. We are called to be perfect physicians, perfect nurses, perfect husbands or wives, perfect business men or women, perfect priests, perfect Religious. As the Catechism says, I am "to do my duty in that state of life unto which it shall please God to call me."

Final perfection, of course, can be found only in heaven. Perfection for us on earth, *in the way,* must increase day by day. A little child may be perfect, though limited in intellect and unable even to speak. But if at the age of twelve he has not grown intellectually and in other ways, then he is imperfect. As we go on in life, growth and change are demanded of us: perfection is not static. Christ's call to us, then, is a continuous call. We need to be constantly listening for his voice. Today I must try to rise up to the vision and the call as I see and hear it today. Tomorrow I must do the same. But tomorrow I cannot rest on the call of today. I must be attentive to tomorrow's voice.

The call of Jesus has come to us. How have I responded to his voice? How am I responding today? How shall I respond tomorrow and to eternity to the continuing call of Jesus Christ?

### The Response of the Saints

Let us think of the response of men and women to the call of Christ as illustrated by the examples of some of the saints. In many ways these human responses differed one from another. Yet, fundamentally, all the responses were alike. All were prompt and immediate; all were hearty, full of trustful love; all were complete, holding nothing back.

#### THE FISHERMEN

Let us think, first of all, of the response of those Galilean fishermen—Peter and Andrew, James and John. What sort of men were they?

They were ordinary folk, fishermen by trade, in a way good and religious men. But they were far from perfect when Jesus called them. They had no unusual gifts or talents. They showed themselves frequently stupid, literal minded, slow of heart and understanding. But they did have energy, impulsive but generous energy. They were men of action and liberal spirit, ready to give when the call and opportunity came. Our Lord took them as they were. He saw their possibilities in spite of outward weaknesses. Jesus usually calls ordinary folk—else *we* should not have been called!

How did the call come to these first disciples? They had the supreme honor of being called by our Lord directly and personally, actually seeing him in his human form and hearing his human voice. How did they respond? Promptly they came. Leaving their father behind in the fishing boat, the sons of Zebedee followed Jesus.

They gave themselves to him as well as they could. Their conversion was not complete. They were not made perfect miraculously, but on Peter's faith our Lord could build his Church, even in spite of the fact that Jesus had to rebuke him severely and in spite of the fact that all his protestations of loyalty were forgotten in the hour of greatest need. James and John too had to be rebuked when they displayed a revengeful and unforgiving spirit [Luke 9:51-55]. Yet there was no real turning back once they had heard the call. Their response was prompt, hearty, and complete. Failure in the hour of trial was repented of and followed by a fuller rededication of life.

### THE LEARNED RABBI

Let us now think of another call—the call of the learned Rabbi Saul of Tarsus, from being a persecutor of the Church to become the great missionary apostle. Unlike the unlearned fishermen, Saul was a learned scholar. He was also a very religious man but blinded by a narrow zeal which persuaded him that God would be pleased by the persecution of heretic Christians. Saul was a bigot, but an honest bigot. Christ can and does call to him those who are honestly mistaken. So Christ calls us in spite of false religious zeal and lack of charity.

How does the call come to Saul? Not from the earthly human Jesus, as was the case with the first disciples, but through a vision—the blinding light and the accusing voice telling him that his persecuting zeal was wrong and not pleasing to God.

How does Saul respond? Utterly, completely, promptly. He was, as it were, made over in a moment. Basically he remained the same person, but all his impulses were turned into new channels. His zeal finds its outlet not in hate and persecution but in understanding, sympathy, and love. Love alone, he had to learn, could draw men to the truth in Christ. He was called to undergo great difficulties, sufferings, even persecutions from others. Yet he bore all these things gladly as a small recompense for his own great sin of having persecuted the Church of God. The vision of the dying Stephen never left the mind of the converted Paul. His penitence went on to the end of his life. He suffered gladly that he might show his love for his new Master. The catalogue of sufferings gladly borne by him is narrated in his second letter to the Corinthians [2 Corinthians 11:23–33]. Can we suppose that, faced with these troubles and sufferings, Paul was ever tempted to turn back and to wish he had not followed Christ? No, he himself assures us of his steadfastness, "I was not disobedient to the heavenly vision" [Acts 26:19]. The vision having been once seen, the call of Christ once heard, that was enough. No sufferings, no difficulties, no opposition could turn him back. In moments of difficulty, discouragement, or suffering, the example of Paul should help to keep us faithful to our calling.

### THE MAN OF THE WORLD

Finally let us think of the vocation of that cultivated philosopher and man of the world, Augustine, enjoying life to the full, pursuing all the pleasure of the senses as well as those of the intellect. Here was a man who was openly resisting grace—rebelling, refusing to become a Christian although he knew that that was what God wanted of him. He refused God's will for him because he knew that the Christian way of life was inconsistent with much that seemed not only pleasant but even necessary to him in the life of self-indulgence that he was living. Those who would follow Jesus must "lay aside every weight, and the sin which clings so closely" [Hebrews 12:1]. Augustine found himself unwilling and indeed unable to do this. Yet when the call of Jesus came to him he found that he must and could respond!

How did the call come? There was no personal appearance of Christ to him, no supernatural vision or sight of Jesus in glory. The call of Christ came to the great philosopher through the voice of a little child at play. From the garden next to him, the child's voice cried repeatedly, *"Tolle, lege* [Take up and read]." To Augustine's soul, the words of the child seemed to be a personal message from Christ. So he took up the Testament that he had thrown on the ground in despair and read the words from the open page of the book, "Not in reveling and drunkenness, not in debauchery, and licentiousness, not in quarreling and jealousy. But put on the Lord Jesus Christ, and make no provision for the flesh, to gratify its desires" [Romans 13:13-14]. His doubts were removed. He resolved to follow Christ.

The call of Augustine was, in a sense, purely natural. Yet it was as truly real and truly divine as though it had come supernaturally. So Christ's call comes in many ways to the soul. So Christ's call to us is truly divine and truly from Christ, even though it all seems purely "natural." Christ may call us through the words of a book or through the suggestions of a friend or through the counsel of a priest—even by seeming accident.

Augustine made a complete surrender of himself to Christ. The sinful pleasures by which he was chained dropped away. "The snare was broken, and we have escaped" [Psalm 124:7]. He knew that in Christ he was free. He consecrated his magnificent intellect to Christ and served him faithfully and unswervingly to the end. May our own response likewise be generous, complete, persevering faithfully to the end of our lives!

The call of Christ is insistent. The call of Christ demands all we have. Our response to the call of Christ leaves no place for compromise. It must be prompt, like the response of the saints. They came at once. It must be hearty, like the response of the saints. They came fired with zeal and love. It must be complete. The saints came with no little corner of the heart held back. It must be persevering. Like the saints we must go on bravely, trustfully, lovingly unto the end.

## Temptations to Disloyalty

How can it come to pass that a soul truly called by Jesus Christ can become disloyal? To one who has resolved to follow Christ, open rebellion against God never comes all at once. Our spiritual enemy begins his work of turning us aside by encouraging an attitude of disloyalty in little things—little doubts, murmurings, lack of enthusiasm, carelessness, lukewarmness, little failures to follow the leadings of God's Holy Spirit. These little disloyalties may not be serious in themselves but, on the other hand, may be the first symptoms of spiritual tragedy. The greatest spiritual tragedy is surely this, that one whom Christ has called to be

very near to him has turned his or her back on him. The nearer we have been to Jesus, the more terrible if we turn away from him. The awfulness of the tragedy of Judas was that he was called to be an apostle.

What are the things that cause our loss of fervor? There are, first of all, the ordinary temptations to the lust of the flesh, the lust of the eyes, the pride of life. A more subtle but quite common temptation arises from disappointed ideals. "Put not your trust in princes, in a son of man, in whom there is no help," says the psalmist [Psalm 146:3]. We are not, of course, to take this to mean that we are not to go out to our neighbors in love and trust. Trust and faith in our fellows is part of our Christian religion and is commanded by our Lord. But the psalmist's warning does mean that we are never to seek to find in human beings that constancy and faithfulness to the best and highest ideals which can be found only in Jesus Christ. God alone is perfect goodness. God alone can never fail. Even the very best of men—the princes—sometimes fail. Even the holiest of the "sons of men" sometimes fall down.

### OUR IDOLS

So if we put other human beings on pedestals, if we erect altars to them or worship them, that is idolatry. Sooner or later the idol will fall, and, since we have centered our religion on the idol, our religion will be smashed too. If we put any human being on a pedestal—such as a dear friend, a superior, a religious counselor, a priest, or even the Church of God—sooner or later defects will be discovered, faults and sins will be revealed, and the idol will be destroyed. And we shall suffer, for we have been worshiping an idol rather than God.

If we abolish all these idols and worship God in Christ, we shall not be disappointed. Christ will never fail us. If our hopes are set on Christ, we shall know no disillusionment. Disappointed idealism can work terrible harm.

The mystery of the fall of Judas can probably be explained by disappointed ideals. He was devoted to Jesus in whom he saw the promised Jewish Messiah. But he was dismayed at his leader's lack of business sense, when he allowed Mary to use a whole pound of costly ointment to anoint his feet [John 12:5] and completely disillusioned when Jesus, after his tumultous reception in Jerusalem, did not go on to seize royal power. So Judas turned against his Master. His ideas and ideals were wrong. But, even if our ideals are right (they can often be mistaken!), that is no reason for abandoning

our Lord or betraying him. Christ himself will never fail us.

### TIME AND CHANGE

Another common cause of disloyalty and loss of fervor is simply the passage of time. The passing of time creates problems for all of us. Life demands of us continuous and changing response. As conditions around us change, we too must change to adapt ourselves to these new conditions if we are to keep morally and spiritually alive. What was appropriate and right for us in earlier stages of development may not be at all appropriate and right for us here and now.

St. Paul writes, "When I was a child, I spoke like a child, I thought like a child, I reasoned like a child; when I became a man, I gave up childish ways" [1 Corinthians 13:11]. But how very hard it often is to give up childish ways! To adapt ourselves to new conditions becomes, for most of us, more and more difficult as we grow older. Inertia and the weariness of living assert themselves. We are less able to realize new responses, less willing to make changes. We try to cling to customs, behavior, habits of an earlier time. We become inwardly aware that these things to which we cling are now inappropriate, and this knowledge induces disgust.

We must pray for grace to continue to be morally and spiritually alive. Our vocation in Christ is ever new, ever continuous, ever developing and changing. There is a new call from Christ to meet every change, and on every occasion Christ will supply the necessary strength to meet it. We must pray not to dread change, not to fear the new. "New every morning is the love"—the love of God. New love is given us each day to strengthen us for the new tasks which lead us on to a new vision of the glories of the City of God.

GLAMOR

Still another cause of loss of fervor is the glamor of the world. If the light of the Sun of Righteousness has been allowed to become dim, we then become conscious of the attraction of outward things. So the flame of a little candle, scarcely visible in the sunshine, shines brilliantly on a dark night. Some of the harmful pleasures of the world, which we renounced when we decided to follow Christ, begin to be invested with a strange attraction and glamor. We overlook the blessings and joys of our life in Christ and imagine the advantages of those who are free (as we say) to "live as they please." So the children of Israel, being led by God into the Promised Land and fed by manna—the bread from heaven—could think only of the pungent vegetables which they had left behind in Egypt! "We remember the fish we ate in Egypt for nothing, the cucumbers, the melons, the leeks, the onions, and the garlic; but now our strength is dried up, and there is nothing but this manna to look at" [Numbers 11:5-6].

So it may be that worldly things attract us when, having renounced these to follow Christ, we turn away from him and let his light grow dim. Our life in Christ seems dull and flat, the life out there exciting and alluring! But the truth is quite different. Real lovelinesses, things truly good, the eternal values—everything that is lastingly beautiful and desirable—are to be found in Jesus Christ.

"All these [desirable things] I will give you," said the devil to Christ, "if you will fall down and worship me" [Matthew 4:9]. It was a dazzling promise—but a *lie!* It still is a lie. Our reply, when tempted in this way, must be the same as our Lord's, "Begone, Satan! for it is written, 'You shall worship the Lord your God and him only shall you serve' " [Matthew 4:10].

We have already experienced something of the treasures of God's grace. We may even have at times had glimpses of "the glory that is to be revealed to us" [Romans 8:18]. We all, in some

measure, have known the love of
Christ. These things are part of
us. They are true and cannot be
taken from us. We must cling to
them, even at the cost of our
heart's blood. Even though the
whole world deny, we cannot
deny! Yet we remember that,
although St. Peter declared
"Though they all fall away because of you, I will never fall
away" [Matthew 26:33], he nevertheless denied his Lord. So we
need to pray for grace to be true
and faithful in the hour of trial.

### Sin

The spirit of disloyalty to the
call of Jesus, if we indulge in it
unchecked, leads us on to sin.
When we consent to temptations,
they lead us into sin, and sin may
lead us to destruction. As we
read in the epistle of James,
"Each person is tempted when
he is lured and enticed by his
own desire. Then desire when it
has conceived gives birth to sin;
and sin when it is full-grown
brings forth death" [James
1:14-15].

In the past some ethicists have
laid down a distinction between
what are called mortal and what
are termed venial sins. A mortal
sin, we are told, is one that cuts
off the soul from God. It kills
the soul. Restoration can be
obtained only by real contrition
and penitence, demanding from
those who know its use recourse
to sacramental confession. A
venial sin, on the other hand, is
quite easily pardoned and done
away with.

To make a sin mortal, we are
told, three things are required.
These are: gravity of matter (it
must involve a serious fault); full
knowledge of the sinfulness of
the action; and, finally, full consent of the will. Without these
three conditions, the sin cannot
be mortal. Holding to this definition, we may very well con-
clude that we have been kept
free from mortal sins. Yet, alas!
that does not mean that our sins
may not be really very harmful—
even destructive. According to
these definitions, the unfortun-
ate woman taken in adultery
[John 8:3-11] was certainly
guilty of mortal sin while the
Pharisees of our Lord's time
(who were truly "religious
people") were guilty only of
venial sin. Yet Jesus tells the
woman that he will not condemn her, while for the Pharisees
he has the severest condemnation [Matthew 23].

#### THE SINS OF THE GOOD PEOPLE
#### AND OF THE BAD PEOPLE

Let us then put aside these
distinctions that we may consider the subject of sin, instead,
from the point of view of our
Lord's parable of the Pharisee
and the Publican [Luke 18:9-14].

The Pharisee, in his prayer,

gave thanks to God that he was not like other men [Luke 18:11]. He thanks God because he is such a good person, and in saying this he was not a hypocrite. He really *was* a good and religious man. But the Publican —the tax collector—knew that he was truly a sinner and simply called out to God for mercy. We are told that God forgave the tax collector his sins (he "went down to his house justified"), but he did not forgive the Pharisee. This is because God cannot forgive us our sins unless we ask forgiveness, and we cannot ask forgiveness unless we know what our sins are.

We must not make the mistake of thinking that the Publican was "really good" and that the Pharisee was "really bad" and only made a pretence of goodness. The whole point of the parable is that the tax collector, who was guilty of real and serious sins, was completely forgiven because he came in penitence to God. Tax collectors were a bad lot, with a bad name. As tax collectors for the hated Roman government, they were doubly traitors to their own people. As outcasts they were not subject to the restraints of social convention. There was no necessity for them to live up to what people expected of them. So they went quite easily to the devil.

The Pharisees had a reputation to maintain, but the publicans had none. So they easily succumbed to temptations to the "grosser sins," stealing, cheating, lust, gluttony, lying. Sins of this sort, bad as they are, never allow a man to think of himself as a misjudged saint. Such people are often unsatisfied and unhappy. They know that they have betrayed their better selves. So they are likely to repent and to seek pardon from God. And they find the pardon that they seek.

If such sins are found in my own life, let me remember that they need both pardon from God and God's strengthening grace to help me overcome them. For those who are seeking to live close to God, sins of this sort are likely to be unpremeditated. They arise from sudden temptations due to the weakness of fallen nature. Falls of this sort are likely to discourage us, but, if we turn quickly to God, God will readily forgive us. "If we confess our sins, he [God] is faithful and just, and will forgive our sins and cleanse us from all unrighteousness" [1 John 1:9].

### SINS THAT MAKE
### THE HEART GROW COLD

The sins of the Pharisee were mainly sins of character, rather than of act, and so did not readily produce shame, sorrow, and penitence. For this reason they are less easily forgiven than the open acts of sin by the Publican. Pharisaical sins bring with them a sort of moral blindness so that the sins themselves—pride, self-sufficiency, contempt of others—are often regarded as virtues. But, unless we can practice penitence, we cannot be forgiven. It is easy to give way to petty annoyances and an unforgiving temper and excuse our reactions as "righteous indignation." Sins of this sort may not be mortal by definition, but they are truly mortal in result. They strike a deadly blow at love. They kill the virtue of charity.

Our Lord, always so tolerant, sympathetic, and loving, uses very condemnatory words in speaking of the sins of the Pharisees.

All the good things they did were spoiled by the motives of selfishness, self-centeredness, and egotism which ruled them. Their own ideas and actions were the standard of comparison for the ideas and actions of others. Anything which differed from them was obviously wrong. That was the basis of their faultfinding with our Lord. They were constantly asking the disciples of Jesus:

"Why does your Master do things differently from the way we do them?"

"Why does he welcome and eat with publicans and sinners? (We never do!)"

"Why don't you fast more often?"

"Why do you heal people on the Sabbath?"

Our Lord analyzes their sin by pointing out their self-seeking egotism. "They do all their deeds to be seen by men" [Matthew 23:5]. They love to have deference paid to them, to be given places of honor, to be saluted as those worthy of praise. Is it possible that some "good and pious" Christians nowadays still do many of their good deeds to be seen and praised by men rather than out of unselfish love of God and neighbor?

The Pharisees had many other sins arising from the same egotism and selfishness. By their harshness, ungraciousness, and narrowness, "they shut the kingdom of heaven against men" [Matthew 23:13]. Those who are beginning to glimpse the truth are turned back by intolerant insistence on "all or nothing." Avarice and desire for money come before the love of God and growth in holiness and real devotion [Matthew 23:14]. Proselytes and converts are sought in order that they may be a source of boasting and self-importance. Absurd strictness concerning minor religious observances and points of ceremonial correctness are enforced, overlooking the primary need for kindness, justice, and love [Matthew 23:23].

"You serpents, you brood of vipers, how are you to escape being sentenced to hell?" [Matthew 23:33]. These terrible words with which the discourse concludes need not be taken by us as a sentence of unavoidable doom, but rather as a needful warning against those sins of pride, self-satisfaction, narrowness, and lack of love, which still assail supposed "good and religious people," as they assailed the Pharisees of our Lord's day.

For we must remember that with God all things are possible and that it was a Pharisee—Nicodemus—who came to Jesus by night for instruction and who with Joseph of Arimathea arranged for the reverent burial of the body of the Lord [John 3 and John 19:38-42].

If we honestly examine ourselves, asking our Lord to help us to see ourselves as we are, we shall be able to see in our own lives the sins of the Pharisees as well as those of the Publican. How many have been the graces which our Lord has given us! How ungrateful I have been to him, how ungenerous my response to my Savior, my Lord,

my best and most generous friend.

> It is not an enemy who taunts
> me—
> then I could bear it;
> it is not an adversary who deals
> insolently with me—
>
>      *    *    *
>
> But it is you, my equal,
> my companion, my familiar
> friend.
>
> [Psalm 55:12-13]

"And as they were at table eating, Jesus said, 'Truly, I say to you, one of you will betray me, one who is eating with me.' They began to be sorrowful, and to say to him one after another, 'Is it I?' " [Mark 14:18-19].
*Master, is it I?*

## Christ Became Obedient unto Death

In contrast to our own sin, disloyalty, and disobedience to the will of the Father as revealed to us in Jesus Christ, let us contemplate our Lord's own obedience. His obedience went as far as it was possible to go—even unto death, the death of the cross [Philippians 2:8]. His whole life was a life of loving obedience to the will of his Father, and that obedience was, as it were, focused in the supreme obedience manifested in his passion and death. "Although he was a Son, he learned obedience through what he suffered; and being made perfect he became the source of eternal salvation to all who obey him" [Hebrews 5:8-9].

### SUFFERING

If we turn and look at our own sins and failures, we shall see that they usually come through our attempts to avoid inconvenience, discomfort, and suffering by any means possible. Our Lord, so the epistle to the Hebrews tells us, was made "perfect through suffering" [Hebrews 2:10]. Unless we are willing to suffer, we cannot avoid sin, we cannot be made perfect.

As our Lord "set his face to go to Jerusalem" [Luke 9:51] to face his passion and death, we read that his disciples "were amazed, and those who followed were afraid" [Mark 10:32]. It was then that he spoke to them of his coming sufferings and death.

"Behold we are going up to Jerusalem; and the Son of man will be delivered to the chief priests and scribes, and they will condemn him to death . . . and they will mock him, and spit upon him, and scourge him, and kill him" [Mark 10:33-34].

The fear of the disciples represents their reaction to the supreme and marvellous courage shown in the bearing and face of Jesus as in superhuman dauntlessness, not in ignorance but in full knowledge, he goes up to Jerusalem to face the shameful death on the cross. Rudolph Otto in his book *The Idea of the Holy* refers to this as a "numinous passage," conveying the feeling of awe, the wonder and fear which overcomes us when we come into the presence of the Holy—of the divine.

But we must not think of this superhuman bravery displayed by our Lord on this occasion as an overpowering of his humanity by his divinity, as a sort of divine intoxication whereby his sacred humanity is overpowered by the divine Spirit, so as to make his human will nonactive. If our Lord's human will on this occasion was simply taken possession of by the divine, if he were not free on this occasion—as on every occasion of temptation in his life —to yield to the temptation, to refuse the divine will, how could his example inspire us to follow in his footsteps?

In discussing our Lord's sinlessness, some people have used these words, *Non posse peccare* (he *could* not sin) as contrasted with our state when aided by grace, *Posse non peccare* (it is possible not to sin).

It is true, of course, that greater moral freedom brings greater freedom from sin, so that the perfection of moral freedom in Jesus would make sin impossible for him. Yet we must not interpret this in such a way as to destroy the reality of our Lord's human temptations. We must not empty his courage and moral grandeur of all meaning as a model and inspiration for us. In his obedience to God's will during his life on earth, our Lord was not behaving like a model toy train running on a track. He was not moved by a mere mechanical obedience. The human will of Jesus was always perfectly free. It was *morally* true that he could not sin. Yet, as we read in the epistle to the Hebrews, "We have not a high priest who is unable to sympathize with our weaknesses, but one who in every respect has been tempted as we are, yet without sinning" [Hebrews 4:15]. This brings Jesus close to us, and makes his example helpful to us. We must not allow anything to rob us of this comfort and truth.

OBEDIENCE

So as Jesus set his face to go up to Jerusalem, the choice was fully open to him: to return to his home in Nazareth or to go forward. The temptation must have been truly fierce.

Why not go back home? (It would have pleased his mother Mary if he had.)

Why not return to the peaceful village, accompanied by his faithful followers, to settle down in that quiet and beloved spot, free to do good, to teach, to heal?

To go the other way, to Jerusalem, meant rejection, scourging, and crucifixion. Certainly for us to turn back to Nazareth under such conditions would seem but a very slight sin; but for our Lord to have done this would have been flagrant disobedience to the will of God, a choice determined by his comfort and by human advantages instead of the carrying out of the work of salvation given him by his Father.

While he was going through this terrible struggle and when in response to God's will he had turned his face towards Jerusalem, then it was that Peter said to him, in reference to Jesus' proclamation of his coming sufferings and death, "God forbid, Lord! This shall never happen to you" [Matthew 16:22]. Peter's voice was the very voice of Satan, repeating again those terrible temptations which now our Lord had fully overcome. The greatness of the struggle undergone is revealed in Jesus' words of rebuke to Peter, "Get behind me, Satan! You are a hindrance to me; for you are not on the side of God, but of men" [Matthew 16:23].

In the agony in the garden of Gethsemane on the eve of the passion, we see revealed to us the awfulness of sin. Jesus goes to the beloved sacred place to pray for strength to meet the coming trial. Stretched out on the ground in the moonlight, he prayed as he had never prayed before. Now that the crisis was so near, our Lord (humanly speaking) did not see how it was possible for him to go on. All his courage seemed to have disappeared. He "began to be greatly distressed and troubled." He said to the disciples, "My soul is very sorrowful, even to death; remain here, and watch" [Mark 14:33-34].

In his prayer he begged the Father, "Remove this cup from me." In one sense, that prayer was unanswered. The bitter cup was not taken away, but the prayer was answered in that the Father strengthened him to undergo the test which, before, he had felt he could not face.

### THE CUP

What was this cup which filled the heart and mind of Jesus with such terror? What was this awful burden that he wanted taken away? Was it the burden of physical sufferings only? Those were terrible enough. Was it the burden of mental pain? That would be dreadful too. But it would seem that the burden to be borne by Jesus was greater than any ordinary physical and mental pains. There is a great mystery here.

Perhaps through all the many acts of betrayal, disloyalty, rejection, and cruelty he had had to suffer there was revealed to him the full awfulness of human sin. Little sins, done so thoughtlessly and carelessly can have such terrible results! Greater sins have such frightful and enduring consequences! It is all our sins, great and small, lumped together which are bringing about the passion and death of Jesus Christ. The full awfulness of sin—mercifully hid from our eyes—is thus made known and borne by the mind and heart of Jesus in draining the chalice of his bitter passion. No wonder that "his sweat became like great drops of blood falling down upon the ground" [Luke 22:44].

Finally, let us go to the hill of Calvary. All the disciples have forsaken him and fled. His beloved mother and St. John, faithful still, remain beside the cross. Wishing to spare his mother further anguish, he yields her to the care and protection of the beloved disciple. "Then he said to the disciple, 'Behold your mother!' And from that hour the disciple took her to his own home" [John 19:27].

So now it would seem, he is all alone, alone in his sufferings on the cross. Yet, as he had said, he is not really alone, "for the Father is with me" [John

16:32]. The supporting presence of his heavenly Father remains. Yet later on there comes from his lips that terrible and bitter cry, "My God, my God, why hast thou forsaken me?" [Matthew 27:46]. The last support is taken from his human soul.

We who are Christians and followers of Jesus, pledged to take up our cross and share his passion, can never fathom the depths of Calvary since our love of God and our dependence on him and faith in him can never begin to approach the love of Jesus for his Father and our Lord's dependence on and faith in the Father. Even if God should seem to forsake us, we could never experience what that sense of separation meant to Jesus. Indeed we do not ordinarily worry when God seems far away or the sense of his presence grows dim. But to Jesus this sense of separation from his Father was the most terrible suffering of all. No further endurance was possible; no greater suffering was conceivable; there was nothing further to be undergone, nothing more that he could possibly do or bear for us. He then could truly say, "It is finished," it is consummated, all is complete [John 19:30].

The cross of Jesus is thus the revelation and pledge of God's exceeding love to us. "Crucified under Pontius Pilate" is a mere historical statement. But crucified *for us* under Pontius Pilate is Christian religion. How wonderful and costly was Christ's work of redemption! Christ was obedient unto death, even the death of the cross. Shall I not, then, strive to be obedient to my discomforts and pains and crosses? Shall I not be willing now and then to suffer a little in order to be faithful to Christ? Hear him saying to us from the cross, "This have I done for thee, what doest thou for me?"

### The Restoration of the Penitent

In spite of all of Peter's brave words and promises and professions of loyalty, he nevertheless deserted his master in the time of need and danger. There in the garden, after Judas had appeared accompanied by "a great crowd with swords and clubs" [Matthew 26:47] and Jesus had been arrested, we read, "all the disciples forsook him and fled" [Matthew 26:56].

However, Peter began to recover his courage and started again to follow Jesus "at a distance, as far as the courtyard of the high priest" [Matthew 26:58].

He followed Jesus, but for the wrong reason. He recalled, no doubt, his boastful words, and his pride would not allow him to forsake Christ altogether. So there are times when we also continue to follow Jesus, but only faintheartedly, almost in pretence. Like Peter, our doubts, our waverings, our lack of faith and hope and true love are likely to be followed by the sin of denying our Lord.

THE FEAR

Peter's threefold cowardly denial arose from fear. He feared possible arrest and punishment as a follower of Jesus. He feared all the unpleasant possibilities of the unknown future, which might be his lot if he were faithful to Christ.

How pitiful it all was, yet how true of us as well as of St. Peter! Following Christ, but at a distance, almost always leads to betrayal and denial.

After the threefold denial had been made, the last time to the accompaniment of oaths, the crowing of the cock, foretold by Jesus, proclaimed the completion of Peter's failure and Peter's fall. Then "the Lord turned and looked at Peter. And Peter remembered the word of the Lord. . . . And he went out and wept bitterly" [Luke 22:61-62]. In that look, in those loving reproving eyes of Jesus, Peter found salvation. Let us pray that those merciful, reproving eyes of Jesus may look on us when we fall and may burn out of our souls all treachery all cowardice, all sin, all selfishness. Those silent eyes of Jesus will bring me to salvation if I will let them look at me.

Peter went out and wept bitterly. Tears of contrition, following the desire of amendment, mark the second stage in the restoration of the penitent. However, tears are not always a sign of true penitence. Grief is not always salutary. There is plenty of false grief, arising from self-pity or mere emotionalism. The tears of Peter were not like that. His tears did not arise from wounded pride or self-reproach because he had failed to live up to his foolish boastings. They indicated instead a real conversion, a beginning of humility and self-distrust. In the future he would be aware of how he would be likely to fail, without the help of God. Putting less confidence in his own strength, he would be less likely to fall; knowing his own weakness, he would become more truly aware of the strength and power that comes from God.

THE STRENGTH OF HUMILITY

So we too shall be enabled to go forward, not relying on our own strength, but in true humility looking to the strength that comes from the grace of God. "When I am weak, then am I strong" [2 Corinthians 12:10].

St. Peter had to wait for his full restoration, until that morning after the Resurrection when he and the other disciples returned to shore after a night of fruitless fishing on the Sea of Tiberias [John 21]. At that time the miracle of the wonderful draught of fishes had been repeated in response to the directions given by the Stranger standing on the beach. Peter, impetuous as ever, jumped overboard from the boat and swam to the shore as soon as he learned that the Stranger was indeed the Lord. Then it was that Jesus asked him the thrice-repeated question, "Simon, son of John, do you love me?" The three denials must be succeeded by three affirmations of true love. So the chief of the apostles was restored to his office and was commissioned by his Lord to feed his lambs and to tend and feed his sheep. I, too, must hear the same question addressed to me, in view of past sins and failures, "Lovest thou me?"

Do I really love the Lord Jesus Christ? Do I love him enough to trust him completely, under all conditions? Do I love him enough to confess him before men, when such loyalty is difficult or dangerous? Do I love him enough to suffer for him, perhaps to lay down my life for him? Do I love him enough, each day, to take up my cross— whether big or little—and follow him? Do I love him enough to show my love to him by loving others, my fellow men and women? For Peter's confessed love for Christ had to be proved by Peter's love for others.

"Simon, son of John, do you love me?"

"Yes, Lord; you know that I love you."

"Very well, then *prove* that love; feed my lambs, tend my sheep, feed my sheep."

"This commandment we have from him, that he who loves God should love his brother also" [1 John 4:21].

Like Peter, we too can rise on the steps of our past life. Through God's grace, even our sins and failures can be used as a means of coming closer to God and growing in the likeness of Christ. St. Peter, fully restored, would never again deny the Lord. Indeed, Jesus goes on to foretell Peter's martyrdom—that faithfulness unto death—by which "he was to glorify God" [John 21:19]. Then, at the end, Jesus repeats to Peter those words that had been spoken at the same lakeside, when Peter was first called, those simple but demanding words, "Follow me."

## The Eucharistic Life

The Holy Eucharist, rightly understood, forms the center of the spiritual life of the Christian

believer. In it are summed up all
the characteristic teachings of
our religion. In Holy Communion we find the great food of the
soul, the source of all the spiritual strength we need. In the
Mass we discover a great acted
sermon, setting before us the
wonders of Christ's humiliation,
his passion and death, his exaltation, his resurrection and ascension, the coming of the Holy
Spirit to his Church, and Christ's
final coming in glory.

The Eucharist forms an
epitome of the whole Gospel and
a wonderful means of prayer and
intercession. It is a never-failing
source of grace to us as we assist
devoutly, as we receive the Blessed Sacrament as our spiritual
food, and as we give thanks and
adore our Lord's sacramental
presence with us. In the Eucharist, we all offer, along with the
priest, sharing with him the
priesthood of the whole Church,
the wonderful Sacrifice of praise
and thanksgiving appointed by
our Lord himself, "O most
sacred banquet, wherein Christ
is received, the memory of his
passion is renewed, the mind is
filled with grace, and a pledge of
future glory is given unto us."

Along with the pleading of
Christ's own perfect Sacrifice, we
are called upon to offer ourselves
in union with him. This eucharistic offering of ourselves in
union with our Lord should be
made by us, not only as we assist
at the liturgy but continually
through every moment of our
lives. Thus our life should become a eucharistic life, a contin-
ual offering of praise and thanksgiving to Almighty God. Certain
aspects of our eucharistic life are
especially emphasized at important parts of our eucharistic
liturgy.

THE OFFERING

Thus at the offertory, we present to God our oblations of
bread and wine as well as our
offerings of money. All these
offerings are placed on God's
altar and surrendered to him to
be used by him as he wishes for
his holy purpose, whatever that
might be. The actual offerings
made by us at this point in our
liturgy are symbols of a greater
and more complete offering
made to God by us, namely, all
our life, all our labor, everything
we have. We are called upon to
offer ourselves to God in union
with Christ, to give ourselves to
him, wholly, completely,
entirely, to be used by God in
accordance with his own holy
purpose.

In the Eastern liturgy it is still
the custom to cut certain fragments from the single loaf of
bread placed on the altar, one
portion representing blessed
Mary, the mother of our Lord,
others representing the apostles

and other saints, and finally still other fragments representing members of Christ's Church still on earth—representing you and me. We then, as St. Augustine declared, are the bread, the one Body of Christ, now being offered in the Holy Sacrifice. The sacrifice consists of the offering of Christ, our Head, and all of his mystical body along with him. At the offertory, we offer ourselves to God to share in Christ's sacrifice and in Christ's cross.

In the Western use, the unleavened wafers used as altar breads are often stamped with the cross. We, like the altar breads which represent us, have likewise been signed with the cross in baptism in token that we are to follow our Lord in the sacrificial Way of the Cross. So day by day we must live the eucharistic life, accepting the crosses that come to us and offering ourselves in union with our Lord in loving obedience to God's will. Thus the offertory in the liturgy is developed into the offertory of our daily lives.

THE CHANGE

By the action of God's Holy Spirit, the bread and wine, placed on the altar at the offertory, are consecrated, changed, and transformed to become the Body and Blood of Jesus Christ. The change is spiritual, supernatural, and mystical, but, nevertheless, *real*. The consecration of the bread and wine in the eucharistic liturgy should remind us of the wonderful truth that the Holy Spirit, operating in the daily life of the Christian believer, transforms and changes our being into the likeness of our Master, Christ.

In this new and transformed life in grace, we are called upon to bring forth the ninefold fruit of the Holy Spirit—love, joy, peace, patience, kindness, goodness, faithfulness, gentleness, self-control [Galatians 5:22-23]. In the consecration of ourselves by the Holy Spirit, the old "works of the flesh" fall away. They flee from the Holy Spirit as darkness flees at the approach of the sun. "If we live by the Spirit, let us also walk by the Spirit" [Galatians 5:25]. How wonderful and unspeakable is this transformation which the Holy Spirit works within us. "See what love the Father has given us, that we should be called children of God; and so we are" [1 John 3:1].

Even now we are truly the children of God, yet the fullness of our transformation is still not complete. "It does not yet appear what we shall be, but we know that when he appears we shall be like him" [1 John 3:2] so that our desires are his desires, our thoughts his thoughts, and our love the very love of Christ. "Every one who thus hopes in him purifies himself as he is pure" [1 John 3:3]. We must purify ourselves if we are thus to be transformed. Think of the purity of the bread and wine provided for use in the Eucharist. What care is taken in making the hosts to be used in the Mass! Let us purify ourselves as well as we may that we may be prepared for our transformation by the Holy Spirit into the likeness of Jesus Christ. In every true Christian, as in the Blessed Sacrament, there is a real presence of Jesus.

"This is my body. . . . This is my blood." The words of Christ at the Last Supper are repeated over the bread and wine by the priest at the altar, and Christ himself says of *each one of us,* "This is my body. You are truly my members, bone of my bones and flesh of my flesh." Here on earth we are the mystical body of Jesus Christ. "I am another Christ" as I yield myself to the transforming power of his Holy Spirit.

### THE FOOD

Finally in our liturgy, the consecrated bread and wine, now become the Body and Blood of Christ, are given to the faithful for their spiritual sustenance. The purpose of Holy Communion is not that we should receive a small piece of mere bread or a sip of mere wine. The bread and wine are mere vehicles for bring-

ing us the true gift, the inner reality, the life-giving substance of the Body and Blood of Christ.

The bread and wine must first be consecrated in order to impart to us the precious gift of Christ's own self and Christ's own life. So, in our eucharistic life, it is necessary for the Christian to consecrate himself to God if he would bring to others something of the love and healing power of Christ. "For their sake I consecrate myself," said Jesus, referring to his disciples, "that they also may be consecrated in truth" [John 17:19].

So I must seek to consecrate myself to God if I am in any way to bring Christ to others. We are not to impart *ourselves* to others, with the object of drawing others to ourselves. We are to bring Christ to others so that they may be drawn to Christ. The bread and wine must be consecrated to become the Body and Blood of Christ. We too must be consecrated and given to God if we are to bring Christ to others.

"What we preach is not ourselves, but Jesus Christ as Lord, with ourselves as your servants for Jesus' sake" [2 Corinthians 4:5].

We read of Peter and John, after their arrest for healing the lame man and preaching in the name of Jesus, that even their enemies, seeing their "boldness . . . wondered; and they recognized that they had been with Jesus" [Acts 4:13]. Do those to whom we try to minister recognize that we have been with Jesus? When Moses came down from Mount Sinai after talking with God, "the skin of his face shone" [Exodus 34:29]. Do our souls shine with the transfiguring glory of Christ?

Christ has entrusted us with talents and gifts and told us to use them for God's glory and the benefit of our fellow men. Are we using them rightly, eucharistically, by oblation, by consecration, by communicating Christ to others so that when Christ comes to us at the end he can say to each of us, "Well done, good and faithful servant; . . . enter into the joy of your master" [Matther 25:21]?

We are called to value greatly the Holy Eucharist. We are called to great devotion to the Blessed Sacrament of the Altar. But such devotion is vain unless, as a result of it, we ourselves are becoming living sacraments of the real presence of Jesus Christ, for a true Christian ought to be himself a living eucharist.

## The More Abundant Life

The call to follow Jesus Christ is a call to a fuller, richer, more abundant life. "I came that they may have life, and have it abundantly," said our Lord [John 10:10]. So we must never allow ourselves to think that any limitations which our lives as Christians may impose on us somehow destroy or injure the fullness of our lives as human beings. Any seeming sacrifices which we are called upon to make in following Christ are abundantly repaid to us by God. "Every one who has left houses or brothers or sisters or father or mother or children or lands, for my name's sake, will receive a hundredfold" [Matthew 19:29].

### THE FULLNESS OF LIFE

The fullness of the abundant life of those who truly give themselves to our Lord is found in the life of the greatest of saints— in blessed Mary, the mother of Jesus. A humble village maiden, she spends her whole life in the simplicity and obscurity of despised Nazareth. In the glory of spotless purity, she brings forth the Savior of the world, the incarnate Son of God. In all things she accepts the will of God in trustful, loving obedience. Let us, then, turn to her as our example and inspiration in resolving to follow our Lord in greater faithfulness, trust, and love.

The life of blessed Mary was a life of great and supreme joy. The greatest source of her gladness lay in the fact that she was chosen, above all others, to become the mother of Jesus, the Christ. That is the reason why,

as she herself foretold, all genera-
tions are to call her blessed
[Luke 1:48].

We cannot think too often of
the inconceivable wonder of the
incarnation of the Word of God.
God himself takes human flesh in
Mary's womb. She becomes the
living Tabernacle of the Godhead,
the true Ark of the Covenant.
As she sings the Magnificat, her
heart overflows with joy. And in
the silence of the night at Bethlehem, Mary brings forth Jesus,
her Son and God's Son—the
Eternal Word made flesh. The
birth of Jesus, the blessed
motherhood of Mary, brought
"news of great joy to all people"
[Luke 2:10]. Mary's own joy
was to spread to all the world.

Although Mary brought forth
into the world her divine Son,
God did not leave her breast.
Wonderful as were her human
relations with Christ, the incarnate Word, he himself bore testimony that a still greater source
of her blessedness was the fact
that she heard the word of God
and kept it [Luke 11:27-28].
She is the type of humanity that
lives in faithful obedience to the
will of God. So, while no other
person can share her glorious
privilege of being the human
mother of Jesus Christ, all can
share in the joy and blessing
which was hers in doing the will
of God. For our Lord himself
has assured us, "Whoever does

the will of God is my brother,
and sister, and mother" [Mark
3:35]. Christ can dwell in all
hearts by faith [Ephesians 3:17].
Faith can bring Christ to our
hearts, as it brought Christ to
Mary's womb.

JOY AND SUFFERING

Mary's life was marked by
sufferings too. Her vocation was
a call to sorrow as well as a call
to great joy. She had to share a
life of suffering along with her
son, Jesus. So when Jesus, at the
end of his life was stretched out
upon the cross, standing by the
cross of Jesus was his mother
[John 19:25]. As she stood
there, she felt, piercing her heart,
that mystic sword, predicted by
old Simeon, on that day when
she had brought the holy child to
Jerusalem to present him to the
Lord [Luke 2:22-35].

As blessed Mary had to share in
the sorrows of Jesus, so every
true Christian must be ready to
share in the sorrows of Christ and
his mother. There must be the
times of trial, darkness, and difficulty, sufferings of mind and
body, partings from places and
persons we love, discouragement,
sometimes the sense of separation even from God. But the
patient bearing of all such sorrows makes us more like our
Lord. The true way to heaven is
the Royal Way of the Holy Cross.

In such times of sorrow, it is all

too easy to forget the joys that went before. Let us think again of blessed Mary at the cross. She saw her son suffering the death of a condemned criminal. She saw the terrible ending of that life so bright with hope and promise at the beginning. She recalled the angel's words addressed to her at the annunciation, telling her that the promised Son would "be great, and will be called the Son of the Most High . . . and he will reign over the house of Jacob forever; and of his kingdom there will be no end" [Luke 1:32–33]. As she compared these words with the frightful reality of the cross, must she not have been tempted to think it all a deception, a delusion, yes, a monstrous lie? So when dark times come to us, we may begin to doubt the promises of God, perhaps even the reality of God.

Yet the times of sorrow are as necessary to the progress of a soul as are the times of joy. Joyous hope must be followed by courageous faith to carry us through the times of trial and suffering.

Faith can become real only when it is tested by difficulties and doubts. Faith is not clarity of vision, but that which perseveres and goes on in spite of the darkness around. "Now faith is the assurance of things hoped for, the conviction of things not seen" [Hebrews 11:1].

Finally let us think of the glories that crowned Mary's most holy life. Jesus, Mary's son, risen from the dead, victorious over sin and death, brings to men the gift of eternal life. He ascended into heaven to the right hand of the Father, and Mary was called to follow him there and share in her son's own glory, in the consummation of perfect love.

As joy brings hope and as sorrow develops faith, heavenly glory reveals the true meaning of love. "So faith, hope, love abide, these three; but the greatest of these is love" [1 Corinthians 13:13].

We cannot picture to ourselves the glory of the saints in heaven. Our mind fails. It is beyond us.

Jerusalem the golden,
    With milk and honey blest,
Beneath thy contemplation
    Sink heart and voice oppressed:
I know not, O I know not
    What social joys are there,
What radiancy of glory,
    What light beyond compare.
                [Bernard of Cluny
                Translated by J. M. Neale
                            Hymn 597]

*"Nescio, nescio*—I know not, O I know not." Utterance is impossible. Yet the very confession of being unable to describe the glory somehow brings a sense of the reality and wonder to us. We

cannot contemplate the glory and wonder of the Blessed Trinity, of heaven itself; we cannot even understand the blessedness of the saints dwelling in supreme light.

"Such knowledge is too wonderful for me; it is high, I cannot attain it" [Psalm 139:6]. Yet Christ has called us, along with Mary and the saints, to share in that unspeakable glory. Perhaps it is of his mercy that even now on earth, at brief intervals, "in a mirror dimly" [1 Corinthians 13:12], we may catch a glimpse of that glory, flooding our souls with divine peace after some little act of self-sacrifice, some difficult act of real love.

"Beloved, we are God's children now," but *then* "we shall see him as he is." *Then* we shall behold the glory of God, the glory of Jesus, the glory of Mary, the glory of all the saints in heaven! That is what Christ has promised us.

What does he ask of us? A little courage, a little patience, more real love, more humility, more steadfastness.

These are the things we need, and these are the things that Christ will give us if we only ask him for them.

He who conquers, I will grant him to sit with me on my throne, as I myself conquered and sat down with my father on his throne.

[Revelation 3:21]

Ave Maria! thou whose name
All but adoring love may claim,
Yet may we reach thy shrine;
For he, thy Son and Savior vows
To crown all lowly lofty brows
With love and joy like thine.   [John Keble]

So we come back to the simple words with which Jesus calls us, the very foundation of vocation, "Follow me." That is the one thing necessary. That is the foundation and necessary basis of our lives as Christians, that we should "follow the Lamb, wherever he goes."

[Revelation 14:4]

God grant us grace to follow steadfastly. Amen.

Chapter 10

*CHRISTMAS*

> *We are apt to think of peace as a negative thing,*
> *or we dwell on the*
> *need for force to preserve peace.*

### The First Christmas

*Luke 2:10, 14   Be not afraid;*
*for behold, I bring you good*
*news of a great joy which will*
*come to all the people. . . .*
*Glory to God in the highest, and*
*on earth peace among men with*
*whom he is pleased!*

"Glad tidings of great joy!"
Let us think a little about the joy
and the peace of that first Christmas in Bethlehem.

First of all, let us think of the
joy in the heart of Mary. She
knew the human joy that comes
to every mother in the birth of
her first-born son. Our Lord
himself spoke of this joy in striving to cheer the sorrow of his
disciples when they learned at
the Last Supper that he was leaving them. "When a woman is in
travail she has sorrow, because
her hour has come; but when she
is delivered of the child, she no
longer remembers the anguish,
for joy that a child is born into
the world" [John 16:21]. Mary
shared in this natural human joy
at the birth of Jesus.

But Mary's joy was greater than
the joy of the ordinary mother,
since her babe never disappointed
her expectations of him. The
angel had assured her that her
son would "be great" and would
"be called the Son of the Most
High" [Luke 1:32]. And he was
truly great. He did not, it is true,
reign over "the house of Jacob
for ever" from an earthly throne

111

in Jerusalem. The promise of the angel was fulfilled in a higher way. By means of the throne of the cross, he would mount to the throne of the universe. Mary, his mother, had to share in his sorrows. The mystic sword pierced through her own soul also [Luke 2:35]. But Mary's joys never left her. For her hopes were ever centered on Jesus, her divine Son, so those hopes were never disappointed. If, like Mary, our hopes and our joys are centered in Jesus, our hearts can rejoice even in the midst of earthly pain. "Your hearts will rejoice, and no one will take your joy from you" [John 16:22].

Then let us think of the joy of the shepherds. "To you is born this day in the city of David a Savior, who is Christ the Lord" [Luke 2:11]. So they "went with haste, and found Mary and Joseph, and the babe lying in a manger" [Luke 2:16]. If they had not been truly simple and humble people, that, surely, would have been a disappointment to them. They found only Joseph, and a mother and child, a little ordinary baby. But the angel had said that this baby was their Savior and their Lord. Because their hearts were simple and their faith simple, they believed what the angel had told them. Their simple faith was the cause of great joy to them. Let us ask our Lord to give to us this

simple, trustful childlike faith in him and in his promises.

Finally, let us think of the joy in the heart of the Christ Child. In the heart of that little child, who is both God and man and who unites heaven and earth, there is joy. We cannot fully understand that joy. We cannot enter into the full mystery of the Deity, but we can consider the joy in the human heart of that little child. He was truly human, and so he experienced in his birth all the joys of dawning human existence. There was the wondering joy in new surroundings, in the new sensations of human life, the feel of the swaddling clothes and of the straw of the manger, the happiness of resting on Mary's breast and being embraced by his mother's arms, the joys found in simple nourishment and in sleep. Joys in the common things of life made glad the heart of the Christ Child. Let us ask God to help us to rejoice, with the Christ Child, in the common everyday joys of life. We too, our Lord reminded us, must "become like children" or we "will never enter the kingdom of heaven" [Matthew 18:3]. We must have joyous, thankful, childlike hearts.

Then there is the peace of Christmas. In the birth of Christ, peace was to come to men and women of good will—to all men and women of good will—at all times and in all countries, not just to Mary and Joseph and the shepherds. The peace of Bethlehem is the peace of God, which comes from love, from good will, and from charity in the heart.

If we would have peace, we must begin with love. The "fruit of the Spirit," according to St. Paul, starts off with "love, joy, peace" [Galatians 5:22]. We have, first of all, to cultivate love. Then we shall find outward joy and inward peace. Peace is the inward part of which joy is the outward manifestation. Both spring from the root of love, of true charity.

We are apt to think of peace as a negative thing, the absence of war. Or we dwell on the need of force to preserve peace, as when we think of the police as the keepers of peace.

But true peace, the peace of God, cannot be achieved by the use of force. Inward peace in our hearts depends upon bringing into a harmonious unity the various desires of our human nature, which are so often at war with one another. The secret of a quiet mind is found in the re-direction of all our impulses. God made these impulses good, but they can be misdirected. If we are to have peace, our impulses must be directed toward God himself—toward the love of God and the love of our neighbor. When love fills the heart, love rules our life, and the whole man is one, at peace with himself, with his neighbor, and with God.

"Let us," then, as the shepherds said, "go over to Bethlehem and see this thing that has happened, which the Lord has made known to us" [Luke 2:15]. God has shown his love in the manger of Bethlehem, and we can trust that love. Let us grasp afresh something of the joy and peace of Christmas by means of simplicity of heart, trusting faith, and good will in our hearts. "For to us a child is born, to us a son is given; and the government shall be upon his shoulder, and his name shall be called 'Wonderful Counselor, Mighty God, Everlasting Father, Prince of Peace' " [Isaiah 9:6].

## The Eternal Christmas

Perhaps with some regret we might say to ourselves, "How wonderful it would have been to have gone to Bethlehem with the shepherds." But, besides that first Christmas, there is also an eternal Christmas. Christmas is renewed day by day in the hearts of faithful Christians. Christmas is an eternal event in the dealings of God with our souls.

The supreme wonder is that Christmas was not confined to that single day in Bethlehem, when blessed Mary brought forth Jesus. There remains the possibi-

lity that Christ can be born again
in our hearts, that Christ may
come to dwell in our hearts by
faith as truly and really as he
came physically to dwell in the
womb of his mother through the
operation of the Holy Spirit
[Ephesians 3:17]. In several
places St. Paul refers to the fact
that Christ truly dwells in us, or
is being "formed in us" [Gala-
tians 4:19; Romans 8:10; 2 Corinthians 13:5; Colossians 1:17].
By means of the eternal Christmas, each one of us may become
a Christbearer, a living tabernacle
of the Word. Christ in us "is the
hope of glory" [Colossians
1:27].

Through the sacraments of his
church, Christ gives us means by
which his living presence is built
up in each of us. He comes to us,
first of all, in Holy Baptism, the
chief of all the sacraments, for it
alone makes possible all the
others. So to Nicodemus, Jesus
said, "Truly, truly, I say to you,
unless one is born of water and
the Spirit, he cannot enter the
kingdom of God" [John 3:5].
We should think of our baptism
with gratitude, realizing that it is
the time when we were born
anew and the Holy Spirit came to
us, making Jesus Christ present
in us. Thereby we gained a new
Christian personality, which is
the personality of Christ himself.

Christmas, then, is really an
eternal event in our hearts and
lives. Because of our baptism,
we are to consider ourselves
"dead to sin and alive to God in
Christ Jesus" [Romans 6:11].
Each day we must be renewing
this death to sin and growing in
our true life in Christ Jesus. As
we receive our Lord in Holy
Communion, we strengthen this
true and inward life in God,
through Christ. Christ, dwelling
in us, should live and grow in us.
We read of the holy Child that
"Jesus increased in wisdom and
in stature, and in favor with God
and man" [Luke 2:52]. So we
ought to be increasing spiritually
as day by day, hour by hour,
minute by minute, we recollect
his divine presence in us. We
ought to be growing up, together
with our fellow Christians "to
the measure of the stature of the
fullness of Christ" [Ephesians
4:13]. Like Christ, we ought to
be growing in divine wisdom and
in favor with God and with our
fellow men.

In that great prayer in the
Epistle to the Ephesians, the
Apostle says: "I bow my knees
before the Father, from whom
every family in heaven and on
earth is named, that according to
the riches of his glory he may
grant you to be strengthened
with might through his Spirit in
the inner man, and that Christ

may dwell in your hearts through faith; that you, being rooted and grounded in love, may have power to comprehend with all the saints what is the breadth and length and height and depth, and to know the love of Christ which surpasses knowledge, that you may be filled with all the fulness of God" [Ephesians 3:14-21]. The fullness of God himself dwelling in us, Christ abiding in our hearts, through faith—here is the consummation of the eternal Christmas, in our hearts, in our lives, in our inmost selves.

"The riches of the glory of [God's great] mystery" is "Christ in you, the hope of glory" [Colossians 1:27]. Only in Christ within us, not in Christ outside us, shall we discover the hope of glory. Let us then, day by day, live and act in the strength of Christ within us, in the power of this love of Christ which surpasses knowledge. As Mary kept all these things and pondered them in her heart, let us too keep these wonderful truths in our hearts and ponder them.

"And at the end of eight days, . . . he was called Jesus, the name given by the angel before he was conceived in the womb" [Luke 2:21]. He has promised that those who endure and conquer through him are to be given "a new name" [Revelation 2:17]. What is that new name? Our new name is to be none other than his name—Jesus—for he is our true self.

As St. Paul said, "It is no longer I who live, but Christ who lives in me" [Galatians 2:20]. We are "made one body with him, that he may dwell in us, and we in him" [*Book of Common Prayer*, p. 81]. Oh, the beauty and joy and loveliness and glory of the eternal Christmas! Oh, the surpassing wonder of being a Christian! For the Word is made flesh, and dwells among us, even in our hearts, that we may behold his glory, the glory as of the only Son from the Father, full of grace and truth [John 1:14].

## Chapter 11

## THE HOLY NAME OF JESUS

*The idols that we must reject*

*are not made of*

*wood or stone or silver or gold.*

### The Name of Humiliation (given by the angel)

*Luke 2:21 And at the end of eight days, when he was circumcised, he was called Jesus, the name given by the angel before he was conceived in the womb.*

"His name was called Jesus." We must remember that that name was not unique or new or in any way a strange name for a Jewish baby. For Jesus is simply a Greek form of the familiar Jewish name Joshua, the national hero who led the tribes of Israel into the Promised Land of Canaan. By bringing God's chosen people to the Promised Land and making their possession of the land secure, safe, and prosperous, by defeating the hostile tribes who opposed their coming, Joshua was a national savior. He brought salvation; he brought security, safety, and prosperity to the people whom he led.

So this Joshua of former days was a type of the greater Joshua, of Jesus, the Joshua born in Bethlehem. But the antitype, Jesus, is far greater than the type, Joshua. For, as St. Paul tells us, Christ Jesus, being originally "in the form of God . . . emptied himself, taking the form of a servant, being born in the likeness of men" [Philippians 2:6, 7]. He "came down from heaven" and lay in the manger

116

of Bethlehem as a helpless little human baby. The first Joshua's crossing of the Jordan to enter Canaan was as nothing compared with the wondrous "crossing" from heaven to earth made by the greater Joshua, leaping over the tremendous gulf separating the Creator from his creatures. He humbled himself; he emptied himself and took the form of a servant, or, more literally, he took the form of a slave and was born in the likeness of men. "Though he was rich, yet for your sake he became poor, so that by his poverty you might become rich" [2 Corinthians 8:9]. Think of the blessed poverty of Bethlehem.

Having been made man for us, Jesus, like the first Joshua, went on to overcome our enemies, to conquer sin and death and hell. He made it possible for us to live and rejoice in the security of the divine protection, to know the peace of God that passeth all understanding. His victory enables us in turn to win the victory over Satan, sin, and death— over the world, the flesh, and the devil. So Jesus, the greater Joshua, is truly our Savior. As the angel said to blessed Mary, "You will conceive in your womb and bear a son, and you shall call his name Jesus" [Luke 1:31]. Likewise the angel, appearing to Joseph in a dream, interprets the meaning of this

name to be given to the child, "Mary your wife . . . will bear a son and you shall call his name Jesus, for he will save his people from their sins" [Matthew 1:20, 21]. The Hebrew name *Yehoshua* means "Yahweh (God, Jehovah) saves."

THE THREE WEAPONS

Jesus then is our savior in a true and full sense. How did he save us? How did he overcome our spiritual enemies? His weapons were three in number.

The first weapon was humility. St. Paul tells us that Jesus, "though he was in the form of God, did not count equality with God a thing to be grasped, but emptied himself" [Philippians 2:6, 7]. Equality with God belonged to him by right, but the Incarnate Son of God did not seek to force human beings to honor him as they honored the Father. Rather, he emptied himself and appeared to men not in his great and overpowering glory, but as the babe of Bethlehem. God the Son, when he came to us, did not come in glory, but in humility as a little child. "Have this mind among yourselves, which you find in Christ Jesus," says St. Paul [Philippians 2:5]. Try to act as Jesus acted. Try to humble your pride and put away your self-sufficiency.

So too, the Lord Jesus himself says to us, "Unless you turn and *become like children,* you will never enter the kingdom of heaven" [Matthew 18:3]. Our humility must be real, not a pretended humility. Humility does not consist in proclaiming to others how humble we are. Nor is it humble to refuse to recognize real gifts and talents which God may have given us. Humility comes from realizing that all we have is from God, thanking him for all our blessings and acknowledging that, since all these things are truly from him, we may learn in time to conquer that sinful sense of self-importance. No place and no work to which we may be called should be regarded as beneath us. "Unless you turn and become like children, you will never enter the kingdom of heaven."

The next weapon used by Jesus to overcome our spiritual enemies was the weapon of love. Jesus Christ "for us men and for our salvation came down from heaven." He came for our sakes and in order to save us. As St. John tells us, "God so loved the world that he *gave* his only Son" [John 3:16]. God gave the most precious thing he had; indeed he gave himself. Our Lord did not assume our human nature, he did not condescend to be called by the human name of Jesus because we were beautiful or attractive or lovable. Far from it. "Christ Jesus came into the

world to save sinners," and the Apostle adds, "And I am the foremost of sinners" [1 Timothy 1:15]. "God shows his love for us in that while we were yet sinners Christ died for us" [Romans 5:8].

Unlovely as we were, the divine love in the heart of Jesus caused him to love us in all our sins, just as we were, in all our ugliness, in all our repulsiveness. By and through that love for us, he made it possible for us to become less ugly, less unlovable, until finally his patient, unswerving, enduring love made it possible for us to become lovely, even as he is lovely. "We know that when he appears we shall be *like him,* for we shall see him as he is" [1 John 3:2].

So he calls upon us to love one another and to love one another not in the way of ordinary human love, but to love one another *as he has loved us* [John 15:12]. We are to love the unattractive, to be patient and understanding and forgiving to the sinful. We are to continue to love patiently those who do not love us. We are to love even those who hate us and injure us. We are to show not merely human love or human patience, but the divine love, the divine patience, the divine understanding and sympathy which filled his own sacred heart. "O heart of Jesus, God made man for love of us, make my heart like thy heart!"

The third weapon used by our Lord was the weapon of obedience—perfect obedience to the will of his heavenly Father. This perfect obedience was the essential thing in Jesus' sacrifice for us. On the cross, he shed his precious blood for us, but it was not the mere blood shedding, but the *willingness* of that blood shedding which made it acceptable and precious in the sight of God. God took no pleasure at all in the offering of the blood of bulls and goats, poor, dumb, unwilling creatures dragged to the slaughter.

God is not a savage tyrant to be appeased by blood and slaughter and the death of victims. What God desires of us is the love that responds to him in willing, loving obedience, the surrendered heart and mind and will. "Lo, I come; . . . I delight to do thy will, O my God; thy law is within my heart" [Psalm 40:7, 8, cited in Hebrews 10:9]. "Not my will, but thine, be done" [Luke 22:42]. "My food [that is to say, the source of my strength and of my life] is to do the will of him who sent me, and to accomplish his work" [John 4:34].

Our Lord's sacrifice of obedience began when he came from heaven to earth. His sacrifice of obedience began in the manger and went on through his whole earthly life to the death on the cross. His whole life was a sacrifice, the putting aside of self-will and self-pleasing in order to practice loving, trustful self-surrender to the will of his heavenly Father. The cross and the blood shedding marked the fullness, the completeness of this willing self-sacrifice, made in obedient, trustful love. He "became obedient unto death, even death on a cross" [Philippians 2:8]. He was obedient right up to the end, right up to the death on the cross.

As Jesus calls us to follow him in the path of humility and love, so too he calls us to follow him in the way of obedience. To follow in his way of obedience is a necessary requirement of every disciple of our Lord. "If any man would come after me, let him deny himself and take up his cross and follow me" [Matthew 16:24].

In the book of Acts, we read that Peter, "filled with the Holy Spirit," declared that only in "the name of Jesus Christ of Nazareth" can salvation come to the human race. "There is salvation in no one else, for there is no other name under heaven given among men by which we must be saved" [Acts 4:12]. We must love the name of Jesus. We must live in the spirit of Jesus. We must try, in our little way, to forward the work of Jesus our Savior by humility, by love, and by obedience even unto death.

### The Name of Exaltation (given by God)

*Philippians 2:9–11   Therefore God has highly exalted him and bestowed on him the name which is above every name, that at the name of Jesus every knee should bow, in heaven and on earth and under the earth, and every tongue confess that Jesus Christ is Lord, to the glory of God th Father.*

At the name which God himself has bestowed upon Jesus because of his human life of humble, loving obedience, every knee should bow. Jesus in his human nature has been exalted into heaven and "sits on the right hand of the throne of God," which is our way of expressing the truth that Jesus now shares with Almighty God himself the supreme power in the universe. So, after his resurrection, looking forward to his ascension and glorification, our Lord declared, "All authority in heaven and on earth has been given to me" [Matthew 28:18]. He shares with his Father the right to the adoration and obedience of all human hearts. "At the name of Jesus every knee should bow."

#### THE NEW NAME

That name of Jesus to which universal worship must be given is not, however, as is sometimes thought, the mere human name of Jesus, the name of his humiliation upon earth. It is rather the *new* name bestowed on him by the Father when, having completed and consummated the work of man's salvation entrusted to him by his Father, he was received up into glory by means of his mighty resurrection and wondrous ascension. This new name, at which all knees should bow, is LORD: Lord, meaning supreme ruler, supreme master of the lives and hearts of men and women. Jesus in his glorified humanity, shares with God the Father himself the rule and dominion over all creation. So in the Apocalypse, the symbolic rider on the white horse was "called The Word of God. . . . On his robe and on his thigh [perhaps, better, "on his sword"] he has a name inscribed KING OF KINGS AND LORD OF LORDS" [Revelation 19:11–16].

To recognize that Jesus, the babe of Bethlehem and the carpenter of Nazareth, is truly King of kings and Lord of lords requires genuine Christian faith, and this faith itself is the gift of God. "No one can say 'Jesus is Lord,'" St. Paul tells us, "except by the Holy Spirit" [1 Corinthians 12:3]. To proclaim Jesus as Lord, to worship Jesus as Lord, to accept Jesus as truly Lord— the ruler and governor of our hearts and minds and lives—these are the things that mark the true Christian.

THE CONVERSION

Really to accept Jesus as Lord, really to bow the knee to Jesus as Lord, really to worship Jesus as Lord—these demand of us far more than an intellectual acceptance of creeds, far more than a formal sharing in Christian worship, even more than outward reception of the Christian sacraments. To fully accept Jesus as Lord requires a real *conversion* on our part, a turning away from the worship of idols to the worship of the true God.

The idols that we must reject are not made of wood or stone or silver or gold. The idols that we must reject are the wrong ideas and the wrong values that we worship in our hearts. Some of our "dearest idols" are self-importance, lack of love, selfishness in every form. We must renounce all of these and give ourselves over to a constant effort to carry out in our lives the commands of Jesus: to put away self-pleasing and to conform our lives to the will of our heavenly Father.

Verbal proclamation of Jesus as Lord is not only not enough. Mere verbal proclamation of Jesus as Lord is completely useless—nothing worth. Our Lord himself has told us as much,

"Not every one who says to me, 'Lord, Lord,' shall enter the kingdom of heaven, but he who does the will of my Father who is in heaven" [Matthew 7:21]. Or, as St. Luke has the saying, "Why do you call me 'Lord, Lord,' and not do what I tell you?" [Luke 6:46].

Those who would bow the knee to Jesus and praise his holy name must continually be endeavoring to follow the steps of his most holy life.

The name of exaltation—LORD —was bestowed by the Father on Jesus only when he was taken up into glory. But, long before the babe of Bethlehem had ever appeared on earth, a Hebrew prophet looked forward to the hoped-for King of the Jews, the expected Messiah, the one appointed and anointed by God to rule and govern his people. The prophet had some strange and wonderful words to say concerning the birth of this long-expected king and ruler. Indeed this prophecy appears baffling in its wording, so strange in its meaning that it seems hardly possible that such a description could be an authentic part of Jewish scripture. But scholars are all agreed that this astonishing prophecy of Isaiah is a genuine part of the text. I quote first of all these words of prophecy [Isaiah 9:6] in a translation or interpretation made by a well-known American Jewish scholar, Professor Sheldon H. Blank of the Hebrew-Union College in Cincinnati:

For a child will be born to us,
A son given to us.
And the government will be
    upon his shoulders;
And this will be his name:
Wondrous Counselor, God-like
    Hero,
Father Forever, Prince of Peace*

The translation "God-like Hero" as given above is usually more literally translated as "Mighty God." That is the translation given in our familiar King James Version as well as in the (Roman Catholic) *The Jerusalem Bible,* where the final lines run:

This is the name they give him:
Wonder-Counsellor, Mighty-
    God,
Eternal-Father, Prince-of-Peace.

Even in the translation of Professor Blank, the name of the promised child is wonderful and astonishing enough.

The titles given in Isaiah's prophecy include those attributes that are contained in the name that the heavenly Father bestowed on the glorified Jesus, the name of LORD, the name which is above every name, the name at which every knee should bow.

*Sheldon H. Blank, *Prophetic Faith in Isaiah,* page 163. Used by permission of Harper & Row, Publishers, Inc., New York.

"Every tongue should confess that Jesus Christ is Lord to the glory of God the Father."

He is our Wondrous Counselor, for he teaches us the way of salvation. His teaching and his counsel will endure forever, unlike the teaching of mere human teachers. So he proclaims, "Heaven and earth will pass away, but my words will not pass away" [Matthew 24:35]. Again in the Sermon on the Mount, "Every one then who hears these words of mine and does them will be like a wise man who built his house upon the rock" [Matthew 7:24].

He is our Godlike Hero, or, rather, he is our Mighty God himself. Jesus is truly Godlike. We look at him and at his life on earth. From this we derive our truest and fullest conception of what God is like. So he can say to Philip, "He who has seen me has seen the Father" [John 14:9]. We cannot have any deeper knowledge of God than can be found by looking unto Jesus.

He is our Father Forever—the Everlasting Father, the Eternal Father. He is always at hand, always available, always ready to help. Jesus our Lord continually watches over us. So he tells us, "Where two or three are gathered in my name, there am I in the midst of them" [Matthew 18:20]. We know of his presence with us in the Blessed Sacrament, but we must not forget that, whenever we are gathered together in his name, he is also with us, in our very midst, as he was in the midst of his disciples on that Easter evening when they were gathered together behind locked doors in fear of their enemies. He said to them then, "Peace be with you" [John 20:19]. So likewise he comes into our midst, bringing harmony, love, and peace.

Always and forever he is our Father, our guardian. "Lo, I am with you always, to the close of the age" [Matthew 28:20]. By means of the coming of the Holy Spirit to us, Jesus himself returns to us, borne as it were on the wings of the Spirit, to dwell with us, to tabernacle in our hearts even as in the Blessed Sacrament. He watches over us always; he protects us always; he guides us always with a fatherlike love—if we will let him guide us.

He is also the Prince of Peace. For, with Jesus the Lord in our hearts, peace will reign in our lives. "Peace I leave with you; my peace I give to you; not as the world gives do I give to you" [John 14:27]. The so-called peace which the world can give us is easily destroyed. But the peace of God, which is the peace of Jesus the Lord, passes all understanding, is beyond human understanding since it is the divine peace, the Godlike peace, proceeding from that love which brought Jesus to earth for us sinners.

Jesus' peace is to be our peace. We must look to him for that peace; we must look to him to overcome our troubles; we must look to him to draw us all together in love. We must expect to find troubles and difficulties in our lives as Christians, things that disturb and worry us. But these are not unconquerable if we can learn to rest in the peace of Jesus. "I have said this to you," he said, "that in me you may have peace. In the world you have tribulation; but be of good cheer, I have overcome the world" [John 16:33].

So to the Holy Name of Jesus, now exalted into great glory as our Lord and God, be all honor, thanks, praise, and adoration, now and forever, and to ages of ages.  Amen.